Behind the Goal 2
An Ethnography of the National Women's Soccer League
Joseph C Wilson

Special Thanks

To all the amazing athletes who have played, currently play, and will one day play for Reign FC; I owe you an unplayable debt of gratitude. (Though hopefully this book is good enough.) I also owe a huge thank you to artist Amy Camber who gave me permission (and blessings!) to use her incredible artwork in these pages.

A note about researcher bias…

As an anthropologist, I am required to learn to see the world through the eyes of the subjects I research. Reign FC fans especially- as you will learn through this book- have a bit of a rivalry with the Portland Thorns FC. I will often depict the Thorns team from the point-of-view of a Reign FC fan, so I encourage any reader to check my sources on any information about the rival team; and I highly recommend any reader also read Gwendolyn Oxenham's *Under the Lights and Into the Dark* that provides a Portland Thorns FC point-of-view on the National Women's Soccer League.

Chapter 1: Indoctrination into the Cult of Soccer

"One Touch" Jess Glynne, Jax Jones

I always believed in fairytales. As a child when other kids were reading *The Hardy Boys*, I was reading about Irish and Norse Mythology, Aesop's Fables, East African folktales, and stories of quixotic proportions. From an early age, my aspirations in life often exceeded what most people would call "non-fiction" and "achievable." There was always a lingering voice that told me to believe in the impossible. I think this is what led to my indoctrination into the "cult" of the Reign.

Reality however often played the antagonist. Every time I found a dream or set a goal of what I wanted to make a career of, places I wanted to visit, or things I wanted to experience; I somehow found those goals just a step out of reach. I never became an Eagle Scout, never competed in the Olympics, never become a lawyer, (never got a date to prom…), etc. At some point a sane person would eventually give up on the impossible. Then again, I was never accused of being a sane person. Even if not in the way I imagined it, I always found a way to achieve the goals I set high on my priority lists.

In college, I made it through flood-level rain weather to get to New Orleans to see my favorite musician live in concert. (I'm talking about you, Kina Grannis!) I managed to convince my history professor to let me write my senior seminar on the history of vampire mythology. (I'm talking about you, Dr. Sramrek!) I even managed to get an Olympic athlete to come to our university's fencing club for a special guest instructor's class. (I'm talking about you, Nicole Ross!) Over the years, I often found myself believing more and more in some outside force pulling the strings of the world to push me in the direction in which I live my life now.

I never would have imagined as a child that I would become an anthropologist of women's sports. And yet in hindsight, there was a lot of foreshadowing. I've been an athlete my whole life- starting with soccer and including a list so long I usually forget some of the sports I did. When I was a teenager, I went to a Boy Scout Jamboree where a sports commentator gave a talk on how amazing a career he had. In college; I ended up studying anthropology as a second thought, became a board member on Southern Illinois University's Sports Club Counsel simply out of a desire to get direct access to decision-makers for my fencing club, and- most importantly- one live soccer game I watched in the summer of 2014.

When I graduated from SIU in May of 2014, I found myself without any job prospects. I applied for probably a hundred jobs- and that's not an overstatement. I think I heard back from two of them and didn't get either. My sister had spent a year in a volunteer program in Sitka, Alaska and offered to put a good word in for me if I applied. Without any other options, I took her up on the offer. Something else that happened in May of that year was that I learned about the National Women's Soccer League.

I had already learned of the US Women's National Team from the 2012 London Olympics, so I was excited to learn the majority of the players I knew played on one team (Hope Solo, Megan Rapinoe, and Sydney Leroux). So, out of convenience, I started watching YouTube live videos of Seattle Reign FC games. After the first month, I was hooked. When I learned I got the job with the volunteer program in Alaska, I planned my flight schedule to Sitka to line up with a home game for the Reign so I could watch a live match. So, in late July I left the Midwest and headed for Seattle.

I remember the game well. The Reign played the Chicago Red Stars in a 0-0 draw. I remember eating pizza from one of the concession stands. I still have the game program in my box of favorite things. (Cue the *Sound of Music* soundtrack.) I sat in the Lower Grandstands and could see the stray unbleached hairs on Megan Rapinoe's head. It rained just before the start of the first half. I definitely remember the sea birds that would swoop down onto the field at halftime. I also remember feeling that I needed to see more.

When I arrived in Alaska, I found out the 2015 FIFA Women's World Cup would be in Canada, and- before the end of the year- I already had my stadium and plane tickets for Vancouver to watch my favorite players compete at the international level. I bought my first Reign jersey (Hope Solo) in October of 2014. I watched the season opener for 2015. I started following all of the team's players on social media. After the World Cup- where I got to see the world's top female soccer players compete live and published *Behind the Goal*- I wanted to write more about women's sports. It was as if I was drawn into the raging waters of river rapids, and the proverbial water of life was pulling me downriver to a location to which I had no plan in going.

Between 2014 and 2018, I had published five books on the anthropology of women's sports. I wrote about soccer, rodeo, fencing, and surfing. I traveled to Canada, went on an adventure across the American West, explored Central Europe, and sat on beaches in California and Hawaii- all to write about women's sports around the world. It was never glamorous though (except that one time I got upgraded to first class for my flight to Europe). I make almost no money from my books, and- during the first three years- I often thought about quitting and accepting a desk job somewhere that actually offers healthcare benefits.

Every season I watched the Reign FC, I bought a new jersey. I now have a collection including jerseys for Hope Solo, Megan Rapinoe, Haley Kopmeyer, Beverley Yanez, and Carson Pickett. One day this summer when my aunt and uncle were visiting my sister and I in Sitka, I sat down with the two in my apartment for coffee. I spent the whole time pointing out the cool trinkets and artifacts I've collected over the years- a Tyler Wright surfboard, Nicole Ross Olympic polo, newspapers from the Fencing World Championship, and finally my Reign FC jerseys.

I remember pausing after taking a sip of coffee and uttering, "I don't really make any money from any of this though."

My uncle responded almost immediately, "Well, you're not allowed to quit. This is too cool."

I laughed pretty hard in response. Sometimes I look back at the moments where I could have quit and taken better jobs (with healthcare benefits) and ask myself why I kept going- why I continued to write these books when I really was not making enough to even pay my rent. (2017/18 was a rough year for rent payments.) There was one day where I was watching the film *The Curious Case of Benjamin Button*. I will likely cite the movie often in this book, but the short version was that it made me think about if I could go back in time to that kindling moment at that first Reign game in 2014. If I never went to the game, I would not be the person I am today.

If I never went, I would probably be a teacher right now, with benefits and retirement money. I would probably have money saved away, and I may have even bought a house. (I know all of this because the person I volunteered with at my service site has all of that now.) I also would not have a wall full of Reign jerseys; a two-time world champion surfer's shortboard; or the memories of sleeping in a castle in Italy, meeting a soccer coach in Vancouver, dancing to a purple-painted singer in California, or waking up to the sun rising over the Rocky Mountains. If I could go back, I wouldn't change a thing.

The Seattle Reign made me who I am today, and I am *finally* writing the book I owe the team. I may not have money or medical insurance, but I have the coolest job in the world because of that one fateful Reign game. For that reason- and more- I will always be a Reign fan. Also, painting with Beverly Yanez and Nahomi Kawasumi in the summer of 2016 helped. (More on that later.)

"Rushing Back" Flume, Vera Blue

But enough about why I am a Reign Fan. The more important part of this book is why those sorry souls reading this mediocre anthropologist's book should *also* be Reign Fans. In the 2018 Season of the National Women's Soccer League, there were nine total teams. Throughout the history of the league however there have been quite a few. In the inaugural 2013 season, the seven teams in the league were the Western New York Flash, the Boston Breakers, Sky Blue FC in New Jersey, the Chicago Red Stars, FC Kansas City, the Portland Thorns, and the Seattle Reign.

In 2014, the Houston Dash joined the league as the eighth team. In 2015, those teams remained the same. In 2016, Florida gained a team in the form of the Orlando Pride. In 2017, the Western New York Flash moved to North Carolina and became the North Carolina Courage. In 2018, the Boston Breakers folded and FC Kansas City moved to Utah to become the Utah Royals.

I generally encourage most people to find their team the way I found my own. I looked at the national team members that I followed from the Olympic and World Cup rosters and picked the team with the larger number of my favorite players on the team. That opened me up to learning more about the "non-allocated" (or non-national team players) on the team, which led to getting excited about the drafts.

I also encourage people to find their closest team and follow them. Going to live games as often as a person can has a massive impact on the success of a team. Apart from having my favorite players, Seattle was also the closest team to Alaska, and I often flew through Seattle anytime I went anywhere in the world. That meant it was convenient for me to go to Reign games.

One big reason I think the Reign are the *best* team to watch though is because I believe the team perfectly represents the league. The team gets about an average number of fans watching games in-person relative to the league. The team has a good mix of US and non-US players. The team balances a combination of national team players from several countries (such as staples Jess Fishlock and Nahomi Kawasumi) with strong non-allocated players (like Beverly Yanez and Lauren Barnes). Ultimately the Reign are a great team to become a fan of for a reason why I love most of my favorite teams in sports.

Growing up in St. Louis, I often watched Cardinals baseball. The Cardinals did not focus on getting the biggest names in the sport. Instead, it was common for the team to get players no one had ever heard of so that they could invest in the player and train them to become famous for their advanced athleticism. That form of team building stuck with me, so I often look for teams and athletes few people have heard of but who equally have serious potential. The Reign are one of those teams that often invest in the unknown and turn them into famous athletes. So if a person becomes a fan of the Reign, they will be able to brag about knowing [insert champion soccer player's name here] before anyone outside of the Reign fan base knew who they were.

Some great examples of these players include Haley Kopmeyer, Carson Pickett, Merritt Mathias, and Kaylyn Kyle. (If you are reading this and you do not know these players, fear not. I will be talking about each one of them in these pages.) Apart from building amazing athletes, what this style of teambuilding does is allow fans to slowly learn about the players' personal backgrounds.

Fans can watch players like Elli Reed grow and players like Keelin Winters become leaders. That way, in the rare cases that longtime Reign players leave and go to other teams- like Rachel Corsie or Diana Matheson- the fans keep up with those players from time to time. (I often send Carson Pickett tweets from time to time to make sure Orlando is giving her enough donuts.) That leads toward rooting for the Reign, but cheering for every team.

I spent a lot of time with Reign fans for research for this book. I never once heard anything negative about players who left the team for other teams. I heard things instead like, "She's doing great with North Carolina!" or "Orlando is giving her a lot more playing time, which is definitely what she deserves." The only time anyone ever has anything negative to say is in relation to the Portland Thorns- Seattle's biggest rival (which I will definitely address at large in these pages later on). But even then, at the heart of it, that rivalry is innocent fun.

I actually think the biggest rivalry between two fans from these two teams is between myself and a sports writer named Gwendolyn Oxenham (aka Doc Ox- a nickname I created). Doc actually wrote an incredible book on the NWSL that I always tell people to read called *Under the Lights and Into the Dark*. The book tells the stories of various women involved with soccer across the world and is one of the best non-fiction books I have ever read. The only problem is that Doc's favorite team is Portland.

During my research, it was important for me to engage in "participant observation," so I started making bets with Oxenham during my study. In Seattle, a donut chain called Top Pot Donuts started making Seattle Reign themed donuts available on Reign game days in 2017 and continuing through 2018. In Portland, a particular cidery began making a Thorns themed cider.

Naturally I called Oxenham out as a true anthropologist/Reign fan and made bets that every time our two teams played each other. If Seattle won she would need to eat a Reign donut, and if Portland won I would need to drink a Thorns cider. (Oxenham 3- Wilson 2.) In true Reign fan fashion though, I actually told Oxenham I would buy her both of the donuts she has to eat per the bets. (You let me know when you get to Seattle, Doc!)

Now here at the end of this introduction, I'm left with the task of finalizing my attempt at convincing whoever has read this far as to why they should continue reading. The truth of it is not that this book is some groundbreaking study in anthropology. I will not be comparing the traveling of players to nomadic Denisovians. I won't be delving into how the diets of athletes has affected their bone development or uncovering artifacts of past women's soccer leagues.

There won't even be a detailed description of the lingo soccer players use and how that impacts their everyday lives. Instead, this book will simply detail the human beings that made the league a success.

I often feel 21st Century anthropology forgets that a culture is made up of individuals. Each one of the seven billion (plus some) of us has dreams in life. We laugh and cry. We dance and make music. So when I sat down before beginning the research for this study, I remembered something my mom actually told me. "Make it about the people," she said one day after reading one of my books. "Statistics are fine and all, but people's lives matter more than the numbers applied to them."

I think that's what anthropology was always meant to be. A scientific study devoted to harnessing the power of empathy to bring us all a little closer together. The motto of American Anthropology is "Make the Strange Familiar and the Familiar Strange," meaning it is the role of an anthropologist to take social situations and rituals some might deem "odd" and explain them in a way that anyone can understand- as well as to take the everyday situations in our own lives and help each other see how absurd our own behaviors can be. So- if I do this correctly- I hope whoever reads this learns about the lives of these players, learns to see the world through their eyes, and finds a team they can identify with. (But actually, I hope they become Reign fans.)

Chapter 2: Coming of Age in Seattle

"Show Me Love" Robin S

Two attempted leagues for professional women's soccer preceded the contemporary National Women's Soccer League. The first of these was the Women's United Soccer Association, which held its inaugural season in 2001. Eight total teams existed within the league with clubs in Atlanta, Boston, San Francisco, North Carolina, New York, Philadelphia, San Diego, and Washington DC. The first season of the league was highly televised with several television networks and companies investing in the team such as Comcast and Discovery. Players received massive paychecks relative to other female soccer players around the world with a minimum salary of $27,000 for a season.

By all measures the league should have been a success, but instead the WUSA folded after three seasons. When athletes hoping to make the 2003 World Cup roster began training for their call-up to Team USA, women who found themselves only needing to compete among twenty-five players for twenty-three spots on the roster found themselves having to compete against one hundred and twenty-five athletes. But while the player pool increased competitively, fan support decreased. The average attendance size per game in the opening season was about 8100 while 6600 in the third season. Television networks slowly weaned themselves from televising games- leaving fans too far away from stadiums from being able to watch matches.[1]

The second attempt at a professional women's soccer league in the US began in 2010 with the first season of Women's Professional Soccer. It too folded after three seasons. WPS's goal was to avoid the failures of the WUSA by using smaller stadiums (to make the arenas appear more populated) and marketed the league to families and "hardcore soccer fans."

From the start though, the league faced low television ratings and attendance. On top of that, one team owner- Dan Borislow- sued the league for anti-defamation when players accused him of abuse and sexual harassment. The lawsuit crippled the league's finances,

---

[1] Miller, Scheyer, & Sherrard. 2018.

and league officials were forced to end the league entirely without the ability support women reporting abuse and sexual assault.[2]

In the inaugural season of the National Women's Soccer League, the Seattle Reign stacked their roster with mostly US players. The six international players came from only three foreign countries with three coming from Canada, two from Mexico, and one from Wales. US based players came from nine different states with the majority of the team from California.

Goalkeepers for the team included Hope Solo of Washington, Haley Kopmeyer of Michigan, and Michelle Betos of Washington. Defenders included Emily Zurrer of Canada, Jenny Ruiz of Mexico, Elli Reed of Utah, Victoria Frederick of Alabama, Kate Deines of Washington, Kiersten Dallstream of Arizona, and Lauren Barnes of California. Midfielders included Keelin Winters of California, Megan Rapinoe of California, Lyndsey Patterson of Washington, Teresa Noyola of Mexico, Christine Nairn of Maryland, Kristen Meier of Georgia, Kaylyn Kyle of Canada, and Jess Fishlock of Wales. Forwards included Lindsay Taylor of California, Amy Rodriguez of California, Kristina Larsen of California, Tiffany Cameron of Canada, and Liz Bogus of Utah.[3]

Hope Solo was born in 1981 and became a staple of US Soccer as a goalkeeper for the women's national team. Before joining the National Women's Soccer League in 2013 as the Seattle Reign's main goalkeeper, Solo already had records at the international level with Olympic Gold medals from the 2008 Olympics in Beijing and the 2012 Olympics in London. Solo played soccer in high school as a forward though, scoring 109 total goals and twice earning the title of "All-American." When Solo began college at the University of Washington in Seattle, she transitioned into her role as goalkeeper where she dominated the Pac-10 and continued to earn "All-American" titles.[4]

Haley Kopmeyer was born in 1990 in Michigan and only played a single game in the 2013 season as the Seattle Reign's third-chair goalkeeper before the team "waived" (a polite wording for fired) the player. Before joining the Reign, Kopmeyer came to the

---

[2] Mandell. 2012.
[3] Mayers. 2013.
[4] Biography.com. 2017.

12

league straight from a college draft from the University of Michigan where she was an All-American goalkeeper. She held records for most shutouts, most saves, and most saves per game.[5]

Back-up goalkeeper Michelle Betos came to the Seattle Reign during the 2013 supplemental draft from the University of Georgia. Betos was born in New York and graduated from the University of Georgia in 2009 ranked second among collegiate women goalkeepers in wins and third in saves. Before joining the NWSL in 2013, Betos had already played in previous women's leagues in the US with the Boston Breakers and the New York Fury as well as overseas with Apollo Ladies FC in the Champions League.[6]

Emily Zurrer came to the Reign from the Canadian National Team. By 2013, Zurrer was already a champion international with a 2010 CONCACAF win and a 2012 Olympic bronze medal. Zurrer too played in a previous women's league in the US with the Vancouver Whitecaps and played for the University of Illinois as well as two U-20 FIFA World Cups.[7]

Jenny Ruiz came to the Seattle Reign as a member of the Mexican National Team, but grew up in California (not uncommon for soccer players). Ruiz had a long history with soccer before joining the NWSL. In 2004, she gave up the game to devote her time to her family, teaching inner-city youth in Los Angeles, and mission work in Brazil. Ruiz came back to soccer in 2011 and joined the second women's league in the US as well as the Mexican National Team.[8]

Elli Reed started playing soccer as a child and continued all the way to the University of Portland where her dedication to the game fueled her success on the pitch. Reed played for the US team in the U-20 World Cup in 2008 and joined the Seattle Reign in 2013 as a Free Agent. Before 2013, Reed played in leagues in Australia, Sweden, and Germany.[9]

---

[5] MGOBlue. 2018.
[6] University of Georgia Athletics. 2013.
[7] Canada Soccer. 2018.
[8] Flowe. 2013.
[9] Valentine. 2017.

Victoria Frederick came to the Reign from the University of Alabama. Frederick graduated from college in 2010 followed by a difficult struggle to break into professional soccer. Frederick played in two semi-professional seasons on the Seattle Sounders Women Division Two team (like a minor league for soccer) in 2010 and 2012. While at Alabama, Frederick played in seventy matches and finished her college career with sixteen goals and fifteen assists.[10]

Kate Deines also came to the Reign from the Sounders Women. Deines grew up in the Seattle area and already made a name for herself by the time she graduated high school. Deines graduated from the University of Washington where she played midfield before playing center back for the Sounders Women. Deines joined the Reign in 2013 as a Free Agent alongside Jess Fishlock, Tiffany Cameron, and Lindsay Taylor.[11]

Kiersten Dallstream came to the Reign after graduating from Washington State University in 2009. Dallstream finished her college career tied for third for most goals for the school and third for most assists for the school.[14] Dallstream is admittedly a difficult player to get information about. Every site Wikipedia cites on her biography seems to have disappeared- meaning I will not discuss anything the site says about her. Even in her six seasons with the Reign, she has played often yet received few accolades in the press- leaving me to nickname her "The Ghost." (So there will be times I speak of Kiersten "The Ghost" Dallstream by that name.)

Lauren Barnes came to the Reign after a phone call from the at-the-time head coach and general manager Laura Harvey. At the time, Barnes was working as an assistant coach at UC Riverside. Barnes joined the team as a co-captain beside Jess Fishlock with a strategy for the duo more in line with "good cop-bad cop" with Laura Harvey stating Fishlock would yell at the team and Barnes "will be nice to them."[12]

The Seattle Reign acquired midfielder Keelin Winters with the first trade in the history of the NWSL from the Chicago Red Stars in exchange for a first-round draft pick for the 2014 college draft and a future national team player. Winters played for the

---

[10] University of Alabama. 2013.
[11] Oshan. 2013.
[12] Christobal. 2017.

University of Portland as well as the USWNT in 2008 and in the U-20 Women's World Cup.

While Winters had yet to play on the senior national team, she was on the roster as a national team player- and the only one of four on the 2013 Reign roster capable of playing in the opening game. (Amy Rodriguez was out due to pregnancy, Solo was out due to injury, and Rapinoe was out due to finishing the season for Olympique Lyonnais in France.) Winters had also played for the Sounders Women, and scored one goal and one assist. Winters left the States and played in the Champions League before returning to play in the NWSL.[13]

Megan Rapinoe entered the NWSL midway through the first season. After winning Olympic gold in the 2012 London Olympics, Rapinoe accepted an offer to join the Olympique Lyonnais team in France- at the time considered to be the best women's soccer club in the world. The club also offered to pay her $14,000 per month- a salary no member of the NWSL received for their entire season in 2013. Stereotypes against female athletes were staunch in France though, and backlash against the LGBT community fuelled the openly lesbian Rapinoe to chose to end her time in France and join the NWSL.[14]

Lyndsey Patterson joined the Seattle Reign as a "Discovery Player" (meaning scouts for the team offered her a position on the team- subject to a required league approval). Patterson had played for the Sounders Women, as well as Division One teams in Los Angeles, Philadelphia, and Atlanta for the WUSA.[15] Like with teammate Jenny Ruiz, Teresa Noyola was a dual citizen of both the US and Mexico and listed on the Mexican National Team when she joined the Reign for the 2013 season. There was a lot of controversy with Noyola's national team status ahead of the season as well.

Noyola had actually played with the US National Team in the U-20 in 2008. In 2011, she went on to win the Hermann Trophy at Stanford University. Jill Ellis- who would go on to become head coach of the senior team ahead of the 2015 Women's World Cup told Noyola to play for the Mexican National Team in 2009 instead,

---

[13] Bird. 2013.
[14] Borden. 2013.
[15] Sounder At Heart. 2013.

and later received backlash for handpicking mostly white athletes to represent the United States in the tournament and refusing to add any athlete with dual citizenship with Mexico to the US roster. (In contrast, five foreign-born athletes represented the US in the 2014 Men's World Cup.)[16]

Christine Nairn came to the Reign from the East Coast where she graduated from Penn State and earned a draft pick from the Seattle Reign. Nairn was among a "core" group of players general manager and coach Laura Harvey eyed for the inaugural team. In response, the player packed her bags and set to work increasing the level of her game in order to live up to the new, higher standards.[17]

Kristen Meier was the pride of her hometown in Atlanta, Georgia when the Reign drafted her out of college in 2013. While in high school, Meier was part of a state champion team and earned the title of Player of the Year by the Georgia Soccer Coaches Association in 2009. Meier went on to play soccer for Wake Forest University where she played eighty-eight games, and made eighteen assists. In 2011 she earned a spot on the NCAA All-Tournament Team roster, Top Drawer Soccer National Team-of-the-Week, and Wake Forest Nike Challenge All-Tournament Team.[18]

Canadian National Team member Kaylyn Kyle was born in 1988 and grew up a multi-sport athlete. Kyle began her professional career with the Vancouver Whitecaps in 2006 and played with the team for six years. In 2009, Kyle played in the Swedish league before joining the Reign for the 2013 season. Kyle earned her first spot on the Canadian senior roster in 2008 after playing in the U-20 and U-17 teams; and joined the team for the 2011 Women's World Cup. She then earned an Olympic Bronze with Team Canada in the 2012 London Olympics.[19]

Jess Fishlock was another one of Laura Harvey's hand picked players for the inaugural season. At the time, Fishlock was already the captain for the Welsh National Team and a major player in the English league on an opposing team to Laura Harvey's Arsenal Ladies. Harvey understood the strength of the Bristol City

---

[16] McIntyre. 2015.
[17] Christobal. 2017.
[18] Marist School. 2013.
[19] Kyle. 2015.

player though, and- upon receiving her new post as general manager for the Seattle Reign- Fishlock was one of the first athletes Harvey contacted.[20]

Lindsay Taylor came to the Seattle Reign after being drafted into the second women's league ahead of its collapse. Taylor moved instead to Norway to play soccer in their league before returning to the US to play in the NWSL in 2013. Before her professional career, Taylor played for Stanford tying for fourth most overall goals (fifty-three) and seventh in all-time assists (twenty-seven).[21]

Amy Rodriguez came to the Seattle Reign in 2013 before she announced she was pregnant and would miss the entire season. While Rodriguez remained on the roster for the Reign, she never played for the team. The Reign had expected Rodriguez to be their leading scorer as a member of the US National Team. Rodriguez's announcement came after news that Rapinoe and Noyola would not join the team until June, and Hope Solo would be out for the first game on an injury.[22] Their only remaining US National Team player would be Keelin Winters- who had never represented the senior team in a game.

Kristina Larsen was born in 1988 and came to the Seattle Reign after playing for Atlanta in the second league.[23] Like with Kiersten Dallstream, Larsen is a difficult person to find information on. Wikipedia seems to have phantom sources on her career, and I admittedly only found minimal information about her pre-NWSL life. Tiffany Cameron came to the Seattle Reign as a member of the Canadian National Team. While a midfielder for her nation's senior team, Cameron took up a forward position on the Reign roster after being a "prolific scorer" while attending Ohio State. In college, Cameron scored forty collegiate goals with twenty-one of them in a single season.[24]

Liz Bogus grew up in Utah where she had a successful high school soccer career before heading to Arizona State. There, Bogus earned the 2002 Freshman of the Year award before graduating and

---

[20] Christobal. 2017.
[21] Washington Spirit. 2013.
[22] Farley. 2013.
[23] SoccerWay. 2018
[24] Ibid. Oshan. 2013.

entering the USL Women's League (a Division Two league) before she played for FC Gold Pride, LA Sol, and the Boston Breakers in the WPS. Bogus joined the NWSL by earning spot on the 2013 Seattle Reign roster.[25]

"That's My Girl" Fifth Harmony

Each season of the NWSL begins with drafts. During these events, teams in the league have the ability to pick players from a pool of available athletes. Several types of drafts exist, but the only definite draft in the league (meaning regularly occurring) is the college draft. At this time, the several teams in the league may hire soccer players in their senior year of college to join their team after graduation. Each team is allotted one pick per round for a number of rounds necessary for picking all available players. During this time, teams may also trade players drafted during the event as well as trade "draft picks." For example, a team may trade their second and third round draft picks for a first round pick to get two turns at drafting players in the first round.

Teams can also trade athletes in exchange for draft picks. Often these are paired in mega-trades (where multiple athletes are traded in a single exchange). For example, one team might trade one national team player for two first round draft picks. These agreements are made far ahead of time with some draft pick trade deals made years before hand. Thus, by the time of the 2018 NWSL college draft, New Jersey's Sky Blue FC had three total first round draft picks, and the Seattle Reign FC had zero. During the 2018 NWSL college draft, the Seattle Reign had their first pick in the third round and chose Allyson Haran from Wake Forest University. In the fourth (and final) round, Seattle drafted Celia Jimenez Delgado from the University of Alabama.[26]

During the first NWSL college draft, NWSL teams had the exact same order for choosing players in each of the four rounds. In the first round, the Seattle Reign drafted Christine Nairn from Penn State. In the second round, the Reign drafted Mallory Schaffer from William & Mary. In the third round, the team drafted Kristen Meier from Wake Forest University. In the final round of the inaugural

---

[25] Linchan. 2017.
[26] NWSL. 2018.

college draft, the Reign drafted Haley Kopmeyer from the University of Michigan.[27]

Due to 2013 being the first season of the league, the NWSL also held a Supplemental Draft where teams could then pick from domestic and international players. Coaches and general managers would have the option of choosing eight to ten players per team to add to the available list- with scouts for each team scouring the world for the rosters that would define the list. All other players found through scouting would be known as Discovery Players.

Each team would be permitted to choose six players from the supplemental draft's list of domestic players and two from the list of international players. Each team would then be permitted to sign four Discovery Players after the end of the draft.[28] During the six rounds of the 2013 supplemental draft, the Seattle Reign drafted Nikki Krzysik from the University of Virginia, Lauren Barnes from UCLA, Laura Heyboer from Michigan State University, Liz Bogus from Arizona State University, Michelle Betos from the University of Georgia, and Kaley Fountain from Wake Forest University.[29]

In seasons where a team is added to the NWSL, there is a special "expansion draft" during which a new team can draft players from other teams in the league. In 2014, an eighth team was added to the NWSL in the form of the Houston Dash. During the draft, the Dash had the option of drafting ten total players from the other seven teams in the league with only two drafts picks from a single team and no more than two US, one Canadian, and one Mexican player from respective national teams.

From the Seattle Reign, Houston drafted Arianna Romero as well as Mexican National Team player Teresa Noyola.[30] The only other expansion draft came in 2015 for the Orlando Pride. Other teams would develop, but because they came from team moves (such as the Western New York Flash becoming the North Carolina Courage), those teams would not earn expansion drafts.

The final form of drafts are "dispersal drafts." These come anytime a team disbands without moving to a new location. As

---

[27] ESNN. 2013.
[28] Boston Breakers. 2013.
[29] Pitch Side Report. 2013.
[30] King. 2013.

opposed to an expansion draft where one team can choose from players from all other teams, in a dispersal draft all other teams can choose from players on the disbanded team. There has only been one case of a dispersal draft so far in the NWSL and came in the 2018 pre-season after the Boston Breakers announced their exit from the league. No trades are allowed in either dispersal or expansion drafts, but teams that move from one location to another may trade ahead of their inaugural seasons. During the 2018 dispersal draft, the Seattle Reign drafted Megan Oyster, Elizabeth Addo, Morgan Andrews, Christen Westphal, and Lindsay Elston.[31]

Following any draft, an individual athlete may choose to not join the team that drafted them. When a team drafts or even trades a player- rather than trading or drafting the human (which would probably be defined fairly easily as slavery), a team drafts or trades the "right" to a player. The athlete may choose to not play for that team, but cannot play for any other team in the league.

In some cases, an athlete may leave the league and play in a separate league in another country (such as Christine Press who left the NWSL ahead of the 2018 season to play in the Swedish women's league), or may not play at the club level at all to prepare for international responsibilities (like with Abby Wambach ahead of the 2015 Women's World Cup). Teams may trade the rights to a player not playing in the league to another team- which can inspire that athlete to rejoin. In other cases, athletes drafted from the college draft can opt to end their sports career following their time in school, and simply do not join the league at all.

"On + Off" Maggie Rogers

The 2018 NWSL season began far before the opening games. Apart from training camps and college drafts, the national teams of several countries began their several-tournament season of World Cup qualification. The first game of 2018 featuring NWSL players representing their respective national teams came in the form of an Australia v Norway game featuring Sam Kerr (Chicago Red Stars) representing Australia along with Elise Thorsnes (Utah Royals) representing Norway. Kerr scored one goal in Australia's 4-3 win with Thorsnes scoring twice for Norway. Elsewhere in the Algarve

---

[31] Bellamy. 2018.

Cup, Janine Beckie (Sky Blue FC) scored for Canada in their 1-3 loss to Sweden. At the Cyprus Cup, Jess Fishlock (Seattle Reign FC) scored for Wales in their 1-0 win over Finland.[32]

The largest population of NWSL players however began 2018 with the SheBelieves Cup where the national teams of Germany, France, England, and the United States would vie for the tournament's trophy. After the first day, England and the US both won games against France and Germany (respectively). Megan Rapinoe (Seattle Reign FC) scored the sole goal for the US in their win over Germany.[33] In England's win over France, Jodie Taylor (Seattle Reign FC) scored once.[34]

Across the Atlantic at the Algarve Cup, Christine Sinclair (Portland Thorns FC) scored the sole goal in Canada's 1-0 win over Russia. Elsewhere, Rumi Utsugi (Seattle Reign FC) scored for Japan in their 2-1 win over Iceland. Lydia Williams (Seattle Reign FC) caused a shutout as Australia's goalkeeper (meaning Williams was responsible for the opposing team's inability to score any goals) in their 0-0 draw with Portugal. At the Cyprus Cup, Thembi Kgatlana (Houston Dash) scored for South Africa in their 1-0 win over Hungary. At the Alanya Women's Cup, Katie Johnson (Sky Blue FC) scored for Mexico in their 5-1 win over Jordan.[35]

On the second day of the SheBelieves Cup, the US and France along with England and Germany tied. Mallory Pugh (Washington Spirit) scored for the US in their 1-1 draw against France.[36] At the Algarve Cup, Christine Sinclair (Portland Thorns FC) scored again for Canada in their 3-0 win over South Korea. Kailen Sheridan (Sky Blue FC) caused a shutout as Canada's goalkeeper. Sam Kerr (Chicago Red Stars) scored again for Australia in their 2-0 win over China.[37]

None of the players in the tournament were new to soccer however. Across the world, young women and girls are playing soccer in increasing numbers, and professional teams often employ

---

[32] Purdy. 2018.
[33] Purdy. 2018.
[34] US Soccer. 2018.
[35] Purdy. 2018.
[36] Purdy. 2018.
[37] Purdy. 2018.

youth development camps to invest in future generations of players. While learning more about the everyday lives of the women listed above would require a time machine, a less sci-fi way of learning more about the experiences of child soccer players comes in the form of the NWSL development academies.

In the Seattle Reign Development Academy, there are four age-based camps; U-14, U-15, U-17, and U-19. For the 2018 NWSL season, individuals associated with the Seattle Reign FC took active roles in the club's development academy. Reign FC head coach and general manager Vlatko Andonovski served as the academy's executive director, and Kim Calkins (head coach of the Sounders Women) served as technical director. Several members of the Reign FC team often came to practices as well to give special instruction.[38]

At its most anthropological, soccer development academies are environments of indoctrination during which children are socialized into the culture of soccer. While there are certainly examples in the world of harmful socialization (brainwashing), development academies partnered with the National Women's Soccer League provide education on healthy lifestyle practices and give those in the academies strong role models within the sport.

Apart from the direct usage of soccer camp lessons for future soccer competition, sports camps for youth also help prepare children for more general challenges in their eventual adulthood. These include how to harness nervousness and anxiety into manageable fuel for success, the acceptance of failure as an inevitable reality, and the value of being part of a team. Camps for older youth (like teenagers) increase difficulty, which leads to increased self-confidence and the importance of healthy resolutions to confrontation.[39]

During the final game of the SheBelieves Cup, US Soccer honored a member of one of the NWSL academy soccer players. A gunman who entered Stoneman Douglas high school in Florida killed Alyssa Alhadeff- a staple of the Orlando Pride's academy program. One of Alhadeff's friends who survived the shooting reached out to Alex Morgan- a forward for the Pride- to inform her of the tragedy. Morgan responded by forwarding the information to

---

[38] Reign Academy. 2018.
[39] Neighmond. 2015.

US Soccer ahead of the SheBelieves Cup. When the US team played their final game of the tournament in Florida, the stadium held a moment of silence for Alhadeff and her family.

US Soccer also invited Alhadeff's friends and family to visit the locker room where they found Team USA soccer jerseys with Alyssa's name on them along with Alyssa's number from the academy. Alex Morgan spoke with Alyssa's friends and family, and other members of the team met the group to give their condolences.[40] While high school and junior high school students had the honor of learning from NWSL players, college soccer players have the distinction of competing against the professional teams.

On 8 March, the Seattle Reign entered their preseason schedule with a game against the University of Washington. Seattle started their game with players Michelle Betos, Christen Westphal, Maddie Bauer, Megan Oyster, Lauren Barnes, Nahomi Kawasumi, Morgan Andrews, Shannon Simon, Beverly Yanez, Kiersten Dallstream, and Jasmyne Spencer.

At the 17th minute, the UW goalkeeper saved a shot from Nahomi Kawasumi. At the 21st minute, Dallstream scored the first goal. At the 24th minute, the UW goalkeeper saved a shot from Spencer. In the second half, Betos made a save at the 50th minute. At the 64th minute, Andrews scored after an assist from Barnes. At the 65th minute, UW scored. At the 69th minute, Ribeiro scored after an assist from Yanez. The game ended in a 3-1 win for the Reign.

The Reign v UW game was not televised, nor did it air online. I had to follow the live twitter feed with updates on the game. Throughout the feed, no UW player was ever named. This was likely intended as privacy for the collegiate players as neither the UW team's twitter feed nor the Reign divulged any UW student's names. I could only speculate over the reason for the privacy, but the simple truth is that privacy is a rare commodity for athletes.

Champion swimmer Missy Franklin became an overnight sensation following her success at the 2012 London Olympics. Upon returning home, Franklin's life had changed dramatically. The young athlete received letters from across the world, but also faced the challenges of having overly obsessed fans and potential stalkers. Partnered with the angst of teenage years, Franklin also had to deal

---

[40] ESPNW. 2018.

with mounting pressure from her fans to maintain her champion status in a sport where world records are broken almost every year. The athlete had to deal with frequent interviews for late night talk shows, photography sessions for sponsors, and increasingly strenuous practices- all to maintain the mythologized image of her "more than human" appearance.[41]

Soccer players in the professional sphere have the support of their teams including heightened security (with some players having bodyguards). Security at stadiums prevents deranged fans from storming the field, and players' residential addresses and contact information are closely guarded. (The latter of which made things particularly difficult for me to try to find players to interview, but an anthropologist like myself has to respect privacy.) College students however leave the game and go back to their dorm rooms, lecture halls, and college campus greens where they have no security, bodyguards, or even parents to protect them.

On 13 March, the Seattle Reign FC flew to Los Angeles to play UCLA's women's soccer team. The Reign began the game with Michelle Betos, Theresa Nielsen, Megan Oyster, Lauren Barnes, Christen Westphal, Rumi Utsugi, Allie Long, Nahomi Kawasumi, Morgan Andrews, Megan Rapinoe, and Jodie Taylor. At the 3rd minute, Betos saved a shot from UCLA and again at the 10th minute.

The UCLA goalkeeper made a save at the 15th minute and again at the 17th minute. At the 52nd minute, Betos saved a shot from UCLA just before Taylor scored for the Reign off an assist from Rapinoe. Four minutes later, Rapinoe scored. At the 61st minute, Yanez scored off an assist from Barnes. At the 70th minute, the UCLA goalkeeper saved a shot from Spencer. At the 73rd minute, Yanez scored for Seattle. The game ended in a 4-0 victory for the Reign.

Preseason games in the NWSL did not always involve collegiate teams. In the inaugural season, the Seattle Reign FC flew to Japan to play teams in Japan's women's league. The Reign lost their first of three pre-season games against Japan's L-League champion team INAC Kobe Leonessa and won their next two games against other teams in the L-League. The Reign were also the only

---

[41] Sheinin. 2016.

team in the NWSL's 2013 season to travel outside of the US for pre-season games.[42]

"Kick It to Me" Sammy Rae

Athletic leagues across the world and across history have traded athletes. In fact, perhaps the strangest trade in recent sports history came in 1890 when an Ohio baseball team traded their top pitcher for the owner of a Canton, OH team to get a new suit and $300 in cash. That player went to the Cleveland Spiders and would become one of the most famous baseball players of all time when his new team nicknamed him "Cy" Young.[43]

When it comes to trades in the National Women's Soccer League, players' trades are subject to league approval. Pay for incoming players via a trade is also subject to league approval. There is a maximum salary for athletes, though that salary is based on the individual and may not be equal to another athlete of equal status on the same team. An athlete cannot be traded with the condition that another player fails physical exams (meaning that if one player in the trade tears their ACL, the team with the newly acquired injured player cannot send the athlete back). Teams may trade draft picks or international spots for players as well. (Though because a team must maintain a specified number of players on their roster, draft picks are usually added to a player in a trade such as one amazing player for one middle-strength player plus a draft pick.)[44]

In 2013, Keelin Winters became the first traded player in the NWSL when the Seattle Reign traded a first round college draft pick plus "future considerations" to the Chicago Red Stars for Winters. Future considerations typically mean another team can have their choice (with league approval) of the other team's players for a future season. In the case of the first NWSL trade, that would lead to Amy Rodriguez leaving the team ahead of the 2014 season.[45]

In July, the Reign traded away Teresa Noyola mid-season for Renae Cuellar (another Mexican national team player) from FC Kansas City. Also part of the trade included Nikki Krzysik moving

---
[42] Zuniga. 2013.
[43] Sibor. 2014.
[44] NWSL. 2018.
[45] Oshan. 2013.

to Kansas City and draft picks (Kansas receiving a 2014 2nd round pick and Seattle receiving a 3rd round pick). Soon after, the Reign traded Lindsay Taylor and a 4th round draft pick to the Washington Spirit for a 2nd round draft pick and no player.[46]

Ahead of the 2018 regular season, the league office surveyed team general managers to ask questions about what would happen in the 2018 season. The several GM's voted on several questions. The results included Crystal Dunn winning with the North Carolina Courage in the championship. Marta (Orlando Pride) was projected to earn the season's Most Valuable Player award. Andi Sullivan (Washington Spirit) was projected to earn Rookie of the Year. The four teams projected to make the playoffs were North Carolina, Portland, Washington, and Chicago. The Washington Spirit were projected to earn Most Improved Team. Laura Harvey (Utah Royals) was projected to earn Best Coach.

Sam Kerr (Chicago Red Stars) was projected to earn the Golden Boot award. Alyssa Naeher (Chicago Red Stars) was projected to earn Best Goalkeeper, Becky Sauerbrunn (Utah Royals) was projected to earn Best Defender, Jess Fishlock (Seattle Reign) was projected to earn Best Midfielder, and Sam Kerr (Chicago Red Stars) was projected to earn Best Forward. Becky Sauerbrunn was projected to earn Best Leader while Sam Kerr and Marta were tied for projection for Best International Player.[47]

A similar survey asked the media associated with the league to answer the same questions. Among the media, North Carolina was projected to win the championship. The four teams in the postseason would be Portland, North Carolina, Orlando, and Utah. The most improved team would be the Washington Spirit. The best coach would be Vlatko Andonovski (Seattle Reign).

The MVP award would go to Sam Kerr (Chicago Red Stars), with Andi Sullivan (Washington Spirit) earning Rookie of the Year. Sam Kerr would earn the Golden Boot. Adriana Franch (Portland Thorns) would earn Best Goalkeeper, Becky Sauerbrunn (Utah Royals) would earn Best Defender, Sam Mewis (North Carolina Courage) would earn Best Midfielder, and Sam Kerr would win Best Forward. McCall Zerboni (North Carolina Courage) would win

---

[46] Lauletta. 2013.
[47] Purdy. 2018.

Toughest Player, and Becky Sauerbrunn would win Best Leader. Sam Kerr would earn Best International Player, and Amber Brooks (Houston Dash) would earn Most Underrated Player.[48]

Also ahead of the regular season, the NWSL showcased each team with previews for their season ahead. The Seattle team article discussed new additions to the team- including the new coach Vlatko Andonovski. For the first five seasons of the league, Laura Harvey (Utah Royals as of 2018) led the Reign as head coach and general manager with Andonovski replacing Harvey after the latter left to lead the new Utah Royals FC. Another important addition came in the form of Allie Long- a USWNT staple that moved to the Reign from their biggest rival in Portland. The article also detailed the remaining core players Megan Rapinoe (also USWNT), Jess Fishlock, Nahomi Kawasumi, Rumi Utsugi, and Lauren Barnes.

The article also discussed the team's low rankings in the 2016 and 2017 seasons along with major athlete departures ahead of the 2018 season. The Reign parted ways with players Rachel Corsie, Katie Johnson, Haley Kopmeyer, Diana Matheson, Christine Nairn, and Rebekah Stott (among others). During the FC Kansas City move to Utah, the Reign acquired Yael Averbuch; and the league reported games between Seattle and New Jersey, Portland, and Utah would all be games to watch.[49]

"How Much Does Your Love Cost?" Thelma Plum

When the NWSL announced the "free agent" rule, it came with regulation and organization. A free agent would describe athletes not yet signed to a team, not involved in the college draft, and not involved in a dispersal draft. Free agents are drafted during supplemental drafts when applicable. Typically a team assumes free agents when they have traded away players in uneven numbers leaving spots on their roster free for more players. In the NWSL, salaries are relative to an athlete's status.

Allocated players (defined in the 2013 season as members of the Mexican, US or Canadian national teams and only the latter two in future seasons) receive the highest pay. Non-allocated players are those not on the national teams designated by the league. National

---

[48] Purdy. 2018.
[49] Purdy. 2018.

team players from other countries are added to this list. Finally, free agents are the lowest rank in pay.[50]

During the 2013 season, each team had a spending limit of $200,000 to spend on paying their players for the season with three players from either the Mexican or Canadian teams receiving pay from their respective national teams and three players from the US national team receiving pay from theirs. After removing the "free" players, each team would have $200,000 to spend on paying fourteen players with an average pay of less than $15,000 per player per season. Pay is not equal in the NWSL though. An athlete's salary is subject to a contract to both their team and their league as well as their status. Pay would end up ranging anywhere from $6000-30,000 per season, with most players seeing the lower number.[51]

The only way I could picture this system in my head was by thinking about a similar culture in history- outside of sports. Because of low pay; the relativity of pay based on experience; and the tri-part status of allocated players, non-allocated players, and free agents; I often think about players of the NWSL like members of the Roman Republic Army. During Ancient Rome- far before Julius Caesar- Rome's army was divided into three parts based on pay, experience, and equipment.

The youngest and least paid soldiers (hastati) stood at the front of battle-lines where they were subject to the highest possibility of dying in battle. The second line (principe) were paid more, could afford better equipment, and had slightly better odds of survival. The final line were the most experienced and best-equipped soldiers (triarii) who rarely saw battle, and instead provided on-the-field leadership and support for forward troops.[52]

A great example of an NWSL triarii is Allie Long. Long joined the Reign after playing the majority of her soccer career for the Portland Thorns through which she managed to break into the international scene with the USWNT at the Rio Olympics in 2016. Before earning her triarii title, Long played in the NWSL by day and underground indoor soccer in men's leagues at night- battling athletes no referee dared card. The aggressive style of play taught

---

[50] Farley. 2013.
[51] McCann. 2014.
[52] The Ancient World. 2018.

Long how to endure brutally physical games with poise and restraint, and it paid off. In both the underground indoor games and in the NWSL, Long managed to earn the respect of athletes and viewers alike for both her ferocity and her respect toward fellow athletes.[53]

In the NWSL, athletes often provide their own equipment; and- while they are certainly not at risk of dying in battle like Ancient Romans- they are at the mercy of trades and injury. Athletes with higher pay can spend more money on athletic trainers outside of practice as well as healthier food and better equipment (cleats). Free agents are often paid at the lowest end of the spectrum- making them proverbial hastati. In supplemental drafts, a team could sign a free agent that cannot even afford to move to the city hosting their new team. Even if they do reach their team, free agents are often traded away for their second season- forcing them to move again with usually less money than they had at the start of their career.

The financial anxiety of the early years of NWSL athletes calmed slightly in 2017 however when Yael Averbuch (then FC Kansas City) launched the NWSL Players Association- a union for non-allocated players. Within the union, representatives of the NWSL's teams discuss on and off-the-field issues with their teams and the league; and find resolutions to major problems. Some of the first hurdles of the union were increasing pay for non-allocated players, increase the quality of healthcare for injured players, and increase housing standards for athletes.[54]

In a separate sphere of the women's sports world, a movement to address unsafe and unprofessional workplace environments for female athletes was building momentum during the 2018 NWSL preseason. Before writing about the NWSL, the most recent sports league I researched was the World Surf League. During that study, I noticed a trend toward the improvement of workplace professionalism and safety for women athletes, so I was by no means surprised by several news stories in the WSL during my research of the National Women's Soccer League.

The first of these stories came during the NWSL pre-season when Roxy Pro (a surf apparel company) hosted a panel for female athletes, reporters, and musicians (Stephanie Gilmore, Lisa

---

[53] Oxenham. 2017.
[54] Best. 2018.

Anderson, Robin Van Gyn, Thelma Plum, Em Carey, and Sam Squires) to discuss the advancement of women's rights in their respective fields. In sports reporting, members of the panel discussed how men with no experience often receive jobs in place of women with experience.

They discussed the diversity of motivation in leading women into their career paths. The surfers on the panel discussed how athletes in the sport today have evolved to be more respectful towards each other, and how more opportunities exist than in the past. One part of the discussion was particularly relevant to the NWSL however. The panel discussed how the "#MeToo" movement has changed their respective fields.[55]

While the #MeToo movement gained fame in 2017, the movement began in 2006 when Tarana Burke took to Twitter to discuss surviving sexual assault. In 2017, the second stage of the movement began when Italian actress Asia Argento revived the slogan to discuss her survival of sexual assault.[56] Since Argento's revision, women across careers have used the slogan as a banner for coming forward with their stories of sexual harassment and abuse- including female soccer players.

According to the National Sexual Violence Resource Center, one in three women in the United States report being the victims of sexual assault with increased reports for women of multiracial backgrounds. One in four girls report being the victims of sexual assault before turning eighteen. These statistics are hard to quantify when roughly 63% of cases of sexual assault go unreported- meaning the statistics listed above pale in comparison to the true, unknown numbers of women who do not come forward with their stories of abuse.[57]

One NWSL athlete not in the league as of 2018 came forward with one such story of abuse within her time in the sport. During the 2018 season, former NWSL soccer player Kelly Conheeney came forward with a story about when her youth soccer coach sexually assaulted her in the back of her family's van after a game. The assault came after years of coaching during which the

---

[55] Roxy Pro. 2018.
[56] Hawbaker & Johnson. 2018.
[57] NSVRC. 2018.

assailant "groomed" (or slowly increased the aggressiveness of sexual harassment or assault over a long period of time) Conheeney in both private and public.[58]

It is hard to estimate how many women in the history of the NWSL have similar stories because of the percentage of undocumented cases of sexual assault in the United States. In US culture, Americans often blame victims of sexual harassment and assault; asking questions about what clothing the victim was wearing, how much alcohol they had consumed, or what they said or did not say to the accused assailant. Even when accused sexual assailants are tried and convicted of their abuses, those assailants rarely serve the full time of their convictions and often perpetuate their behavior towards multiple women and children.

Stories like Conheeney's are not uncommon in US-based sports either. In USA Gymnastics, three gymnasts represented two hundred sixty victims of sexual abuse and detailed their stories in a 2017/18 lawsuit against the chief abuser. For years, USA gymnastics had either ignored or covered up complaints against the accused abuser, and- in doing so- allowed the abuser to continue sexually assaulting young athletes. While the accused abuser received one hundred forty years in prison for his crimes, the several other members of USA Gymnastics that allowed the abuse to continue went unpunished.[59]

USA Gymnastics sexual assault statistics help illustrate how national trends in the US reflect trends in US-based women's sports. While few reported cases of sexual assault exist within the NWSL and US Soccer, there are likely equal or similar statistics within women's soccer. In painfully simple terms; what this means is that before a soccer player joins the National Women's Soccer League, that athlete's life is far more complex than most viewers could understand.

Commonly documented unsafe working conditions in the NWSL most commonly manifest in low-quality training facilities and unsafe living conditions. In 2018, several members of the Sky Blue FC discussed the unsafe working conditions with the New Jersey team. Team owner and New Jersey Governor (somehow) Phil

---

[58] Conheney. 2018.
[59] Perez. 2018.

Murphy wrestled with the difficult task of using microscopic funding to support a professional sports team.

The owner had only $57,400 to spend on housing the entire team. To do so, the owner limited housing only to athletes from outside of New Jersey- forcing some players to commute from far ends of the state to practices and games. Those that did receive housing only received seasonal leases- as housing during peak tourism season for the state was too expensive for the professional sports team to afford. The housing the team *could* afford for their athletes were some of the most degraded houses in the state with leaking roofs, plastic bags for windows, and tight living quarters for residents. Even the stadium had quality issues- as there were no showers for the players and no on-the-field resources for injured athletes.

If a team folds, the situation for members of the team would be even worse because the non-allocated players and free agents (the bulk of the team's roster) would be unable to play professional soccer in the US due to roster size limits. Players are afraid to speak out about their issues as well because the league is slow to respond to stories of workplace unprofessionalism. Speaking out against their teams or the league could result in non-allocated players losing positions on their teams and never playing professional soccer again.[60]

Even in the case of professional women's soccer, victims of abuse and neglect are often the most punished when they come forward with their stories of abuse. Their only path towards salvation comes in the hope of finding a different team in the league that can give them the safety and professionalism they deserve as athletes- and unfortunately that did not exist with every team.

---

[60] Allan & Ayala. 2018.

Chapter 3: Being and Place Among the Reign

"The Middle" Zedd, Maren Morris, Grey

My first of many field studies to Seattle began on 22 March when I packed my bags in Sitka, Alaska and hopped on a plane for Washington. After spending my first night getting to know my roommates at the hostel, drinking beers on a bar crawl, and singing with karaoke first-timers; I noticed a trend developing with my travels. With the comparison between NWSL players and Roman Republic Army structures still in my head, I realized I had graduated out of the hastati stage of my own career path. I was spending time with people from England, Australia, and New Zealand who were on their first expeditions from home.

My first solo adventure was to New Orleans when I was only twenty years old. In 2018, I was spending time with people between nineteen and twenty-two on their own first solo adventures. None of them really knew what they wanted to do for careers yet, and some had not even started university classes. I remember my first book on women's sports- also soccer (and maybe serendipitously so)- when I first left the United States as a solo traveler.

On that first night of the research trip, I thought about the people I met in Vancouver; the former FIFA referee from New York, the sports photographer from Brazil, the soccer instructor from France, and everyone in between. I went to bed that night realizing I had entered the "principe" class of anthropology, and I was no longer a rookie researcher.

There were some serious connotations to that. I found myself needing to raise the standard of my own research, as well as provide guidance to young travelers I met studying social sciences who would ask me for what to do after they graduated from their university. I would tell stories of my travels and help connect them with ideas for jobs they could consider after graduation. My new role also drew me to spending more time with fellow travel principes.

During my first full day in Seattle, I traversed the city with a woman from Russia finishing her last year of college in New York. The amateur swing dancer and I met at a coffee shop and spoke about women's studies before exploring the tower at Volunteer Park. We explored a record store followed by a thrift shop and found strange sidewalks along the way. In the Capital Hill area of Seattle, there are a series of sidewalks that feature the steps for popular dances (like swing, salsa, and foxtrot), so the two of us learned new dances, located Seattle's haunted soda machine, and ate dinner at a restaurant called "The Yeti."

Ahead of the season opener games, Managing Director of the NWSL Amanda Duffy made an announcement with serious repercussions on league regulations. The NWSL had updated their Roster Rules to increase the team pay cap to $350,000 per year (from the starting number in 2013 of $200,000) with a minimum salary per player of $15,750 and maximum salary of $44,000.

Each team would have a min/max limit of 18-20 non-allocated players (including free agents and excluding injury and national team replacement players). Duffy also announced the league had lost two teams (FC Kansas City and Boston Breakers), but was growing with the addition of the Utah Royals FC and growth in marketing, sales, fans, broadcasters, and overall quality.[61]

With no league commissioner, Amanda Duffy filled the chair as a steward (a temporary replacement without title) as the head of administrative roles. The unfortunate side of this meant that Duffy was responsible for the roles of an unfilled position and subject to criticism for filling the job of an unassigned chair- without having the authority to respond to those criticisms with proper action or change. Essentially- anthropologically speaking- Amanda Duffy was the regent for the throne of the NWSL without the power to enact laws or regulations that could improve the status of subjects of her kingdom.

For example, American Soccer Now interviewed Amanda Duffy in May of 2017 to learn more about what the league was doing to improve the conditions of women in the league. Questions ranged from asking how the league was preventing players from leaving to play in European leagues and the stability of the NWSL, to the process by which the league hired women and minorities to ensure equal opportunity hires.[62]

Leadership in the NWSL did not end with the steward of the league however. With an empty seat in the league, the majority of

---

[61] Balf. 2018.
[62] Halloran. 2017.

leadership falls on team owners and general managers. In 2013, Bill and Teresa Predmore started the Seattle Reign FC as owners of the team with Bill Predmore acting as team president. Bill was by no means new to women's soccer either- as he and his wife named their daughter Mia after USWNT forward Mia Hamm. Teresa Pedmore played soccer for Oregon State against famous USWNT members Julie Foudy and Tiffeny Milbrett.[63]

The Seattle Reign team owners are by no means withdrawn from the team. In 2016, Teresa Predmore traveled with members of the Reign to Ethiopia to work with a community of women to improve the quality of drinking water and standards of soccer programs for girls in rural East African communities. Lauren Barnes and Elli Reed traveled with Teresa Predmore to Ethiopia to help construct sewage trenches and wells for safe drinking water to open access for girls in education and increase availability of sports for young women and girls.[64]

Before the 2018 opening game, the Seattle Reign hosted a season ticket holder event to introduce fans with season tickets to the team including a question and answer panel with athletes and the new coach Vlatko Andonovski. A series of YouTube videos recorded the highlights of the events. Coach Andovovski discussed pre-season training during which he stressed the importance of building respect for the game, molding a team mentality, and forging a recognizable team culture. He discussed how he worked on building a formidable roster with the many new players on the team for the season and- perhaps most importantly- the sheer quantity of coffee he consumes in his new city.[65]

With no league commissioner, most of the responsibility of preserving the unity of the NWSL falls on the third tier of leadership- general managers and coaches. Leadership among the teams can differ with owners and presidents often being the same individual (or in the case of the Reign one of two owners acting as president), and general managers and head coaches are the same person (such as the case with Seattle). In the case of the North Carolina Courage, the owner (Stephen Malik) is not the president

---

[63] Brodeur. 2013.
[64] Water 1st International. 2016.
[65] Seattle Reign FC. 2018.

(Curt Johnson). The president also acts as general manager and Paul Riley served as head coach only.

Essentially, owners act as the business operators of a team- the financiers who collect funds from the NWSL and team revenue before distributing it among the staff and athletes of the team. The president acts as chief executive officer, typically acting as emissary for the team to the NWSL. The general manager is in charge of organizing the team and coaching staff, and the head coach leads the team on the field and in training.

To return to anthropological metaphors, if the NWSL league commissioner is the king/queen, a team president is the vassal of each team- responsible for diplomatic relations and raising the team. A general manager is the peace chief of a team- responsible for maintaining the unity of the team. Finally, the head coach acts as the war chief- responsible for organizing the "warrior" athletes in training for competition and leading them during games.

In the case of the Seattle Reign, the war chief (head coach) is also the peace chief (general manager), and in 2018 that role fell on Vlatko Andonovski. Andonovski was also the most statistically successful coach in the NWSL ahead of joining the Reign for the 2018 season. Over his first five seasons with the NWSL (one of the few coaches to coach in every season of the league), Andonovski racked up the record for most championship wins of any coach.

Andonovski came to the coaching world after a career as a soccer player in Europe and the United States. The coach combines strategies of outdoor and indoor soccer to create a highly defensive and technical game, and led FC Kansas City to two NWSL Championships (both of which saw Kansas City defeat Seattle in the final).[66] Finally, on 24 March, the regular season began.

I entered Memorial Stadium for the first time in four years, collected my season ticket holder scarf, then watched the Reign and the Washington Spirit warm up on the cold field. The previous day began with snow falling on Seattle, and the city was still cold for early spring. After the teams retreated to their locker rooms; I watched the stadium recognize the local state high school women's soccer champions, perform the flag ceremony, and announce the

---

[66] Seattle Reign FC. 2018.

names of the game's referees and players. After the national anthem, the game began.

During the first half, Megan Rapinoe scored early at the 6th minute to open the match. Michelle Betos made a save soon after to prevent the Spirit from scoring. The Reign defense held strong against the aggressive Spirit offense throughout the first thirty minutes of the game. At the 35th minute, Jodie Taylor scored for the Reign to make a two-point game going into the half. During the second half, temperatures dropped even further as the Reign offense took early control of the ball.

A Spirit counter-attack in the 56th minute forced Betos to make a save before several substitutions. At the 65th minute, Rapinoe garnered a Yellow Card for an injured Spirit player. At the 69th minute, Joanna Lohman scored for the Spirit to make a 2-1 game. More substitutes entered the game soon after as the Reign recaptured the ball and went on the offensive. Several Spirit counterattacks in the last thirty minutes forced Betos to make several saves, but the Seattle defense held. The game ended 2-1 with a win for the Reign.

I took a cousin of mine who lived in Seattle at the time to the game. It was the first time he had ever seen a Reign game or any women's soccer game in person. The two of us shivered in the cold night, devoured hot concession stand food, and drank fresh coffee to stay warm- and we were not the only ones. The stadium was packed to a nearly sold out crowd. After the game, my cousin and I left the stadium and ate dinner at a nearby Greek restaurant before I returned to my hostel and warmed myself back up.

During my last night in Seattle before returning to Sitka, I sat down for a spaghetti dinner at the hostel. The staff at the hostel hosted weekly group meals for guests with help from guest volunteers in preparing food and cleaning up after. Team dynamic at the spaghetti dinner was equally important as team dynamic is in NWSL teams. A team may have the best athletes in the league, but without communication and teamwork to bind their talent together, the team cannot thrive on individual skill. There is a term in sports (especially in women's soccer) called "gelling" that defines quality by which a collection of individual athletes work together as a cohesive unit- and few teams "gel" as well as the Seattle Reign.

The perfect example of the Reign's knack for gelling comes in the form of long-time staples of the team Beverly Yanez and

Lauren Barnes. Part of their quality of gelling comes from their individual leadership among their respective positions on the field. Barnes acts as a leader for Reign defense while Yanez acts in the midfield to mesh defensive strategy with counter-attacking and sending the ball into the offense. The two players also lead the team off the field in providing strong model behavior for the rest of the Seattle Reign.

    Yanez acts as a diplomatic voice in coordinating strong leadership between coaching staff and players, and is a chief delegate to the non-allocated player's union; while Barnes' competitive play encourages athletes to stretch their capabilities on the field to play beyond their perceived limits (plus she often cooks for the team). The two "principes" also help act as mediators between allocated players like Megan Rapinoe and rookies and free agents in unifying the different castes of the team.[67]

    Anthropologist Marshall Sahlins found a type of leadership among Melanesians in Papua New Guinea in which leadership was not inherited or elected, but rather developed out of a need for unison among a small group where unofficial authority was key for the survival of the group. He called this type of leadership position the "Big Man." Since the term is neither feminine nor related to sports, I imagine I have the right to create my own term for this role in women's sports. (Though after deep thought and realizing I've never created my own terms, I ended with simply altering the term to be "Big Woman.")

    Big Women can be any number of positions on a soccer roster, and there can be a single Big Woman on a team or multiple. However, there are usually a small few within a given team. These are never allocated players or national team members because those players often leave the team to represent their countries (though Big Women can exist within a national team roster). Instead, the Big Women of the NWSL fall within the principe demographic- women with the experience of having been on a team for a long time, but without added responsibility that pulls them away from the league to play in international games.

    For the Seattle Reign, the Big Women of the team were Lauren Barnes (defender) and Beverly Yanez (midfielder/forward).

---

[67] Seattle Reign FC. 2018.

Within the confines of the NWSL, the role of Big Women is to provide moral support for the team during games and to act as role models for behavior for new players. While the more official "Captain" is responsible for communicating to referees on the field, Big Women are often the first to berate referees for poor calls, charge teammates who score goals to celebrate their success, and shout commands across the field to other players.

Beverley Yanez (nie Goebel) grew up in Southern California and began playing soccer at five years old. In 1999, Yanez' mom took her to the Women's World Cup final in Pasadena, and the young girl instantly knew what she wanted to do as a career. Yanez began playing professional soccer in 2010 including two seasons in the Japanese women's league where she earned the Top Goalscorer award in 2013. The "Sunshine Assassin" then moved to the NWSL in 2014 by joining the Seattle Reign and has been a staple of the team ever since.[68]

Lauren Barnes also grew up in Southern California and played soccer from an early age. Both of her parents were athletes, so Barnes played as many sports growing up as she could. Soccer took hold though, and Barnes turned professional in 2011 when she assumed a roster spot on the USWNT. In 2015 and 2016, Barnes made the NWSL Best XI list and in 2016 earned the Defender of the Year award.

Barnes has been a member of the Seattle Reign for longer than any other 2018 player- a major reason for her strength as a Reign Big Woman. Away from the pitch, Barnes loves photography, sports psychology, sharing food and coffee with teammates, and spending summer days in Seattle. In 2018 Barnes was also an ambassador for the Special Olympics.[69]

Lauren Barnes was also one of two captains for the Seattle Reign during the 2018 season. Since the departure of longtime player Keelin Winters- who served as team captain from 2013-2016- Lauren Barnes and Jess Fishlock served as co-captains for the team beginning in 2017. (Typically Barnes acted as captain while Fishlock was away for international duty as a member of the Welsh national

---

[68] Camber. 2018.
[69] Camber. 2018.

team.) Soccer captains act as captains in any sports team with the title.

"Captain" is an official title (denoted in the NWSL with a yellow armband marked with the letter "C")- as opposed to the Big Women of the league. While captains have the official role of representing a team during a game as chief emissaries to the referees on the field, the title also comes with unofficial roles. Captains across sports are expected to hold themselves to standards of passion for their respective sport, courage in the face of adversity, and consistency of play among themselves and their team.[70]

Outside of sports, a similar role exists within the American political system with the role of a Party Whip. The Whip (a term that itself derived from sports via foxhunting) describes a member of a political party tasked with organizing the politicians *within* the party into a singular voice *for* the party.[71] Like with party whips organizing fellow politicians, NWSL captains have the responsibility as official leaders on the field to organize athletes during plays and maintain the overall composure of the team to prevent individuals from incurring penalties.

When I returned to Alaska, I sifted through the opening weekend's results in the league. The North Carolina Courage defeated the Portland Thorns FC 1-0 with Debhina of the Courage scoring the sole goal. The Orlando Pride tied the Utah Royals FC 1-1 with Marta (Orlando) and Gunnhildur Jonsdottir (Utah) scoring for their respective teams. The Seattle Reign FC defeated the Washington Spirit with goals from Megan Rapinoe (Seattle), Jodie Taylor (Seattle), and Joanna Lohman (Washington). In the final game, the Houston Dash tied the Chicago Red Stars 1-1 with goals from Kimberley Keever (Houston) and Taylor Comeau (Chicago).[72]

For the opening week of the league, Megan Rapinoe (Seattle Reign FC) earned the Player of the Week award, Gunnhildur Jonsdottir (Portland Thorns FC) earned the Goal of the Week, and Adriana Franch (Portland) took away the Save of the Week award. For the second week of the NWSL, Jane Campbell (Houston Dash) earned the Save of the Week, Mallory Pugh (Washington Spirit)

---

[70] Blue & Lauer. 2018.
[71] US Senate. 2018.
[72] Purdy. 2018.

earned Player of the Week, and Lindsey Horan (Portland) earned Goal of the Week. Megan Rapinoe (Seattle) earned the Player of the Month award.

The March Team of the Month consisted of Jane Campbell (Houston Dash) as goalkeeper. Defenders included Jaelene Hinkle (North Carolina Courage), Becky Sauerbrunn (Utah Royals FC), Rebecca Sonnett (Portland Thorns FC), and Rachel Daly (Houston). Midfielders included Lindsey Horan (Portland), Debhina (North Carolina), and Gunnhildur Jonsdottir (Utah). Forwards included Megan Rapinoe (Seattle Reign FC), Mallory Pugh (Washington Spirit), and Crystal Dunn (North Carolina).[73]

"What About Us" The Saturdays

April's section of the NWSL season began with two national teams squaring off in a friendly match. In the first half of the USA v Mexico game, Mallory Pugh (Washington Spirit) scored in the 3rd minute after an assist from Megan Rapinoe (Seattle Reign FC). At the 17th minute, Mexico scored off a corner kick. At the 24th minute, Mexico scored again- though this was ruled as off-sides. Two minutes later, Lindsey Horan (Portland Thorns FC) scored off an assist from Rapinoe.

At the 35th minute, Carli Lloyd (Sky Blue FC) scored for the US to become the sixth player in the history of the USWNT to score one hundred international goals. At the 44th minute, Alex Morgan (Orlando Pride) scored off an assist from Rapinoe. During the second half, the US continued to dominate. At the 63rd minute, Rapinoe scored for the US. At the 69th minute, Morgan scored again off an assist from Rapinoe. The game ended with a 6-1 victory for the United States.

Elsewhere in the world, several NWSL players represented other national teams in friendlies and World Cup qualifying matches. France defeated Canada and Nigeria; Argentina defeated Ecuador; Japan tied with Australia and defeated Vietnam; Brazil defeated Argentina, Ecuador, and Venezuela; Chile defeated Peru; Denmark defeated Ukraine; England defeated Bosnia and Herzegovina and tied with Wales; Iceland defeated Slovenia and the Faroe Islands;

---

[73] Balf. 2018.

Ireland defeated Slovakia; Norway defeated Northern Ireland; and Scotland defeated Poland and lost to Switzerland.[74]

Goals during these numerous games (for NWSL players) came from Estefania Banini (Washington Spirit), Sam Kerr (Chicago Red Stars), Debhina (North Carolina Courage), Andressinha (Houston Dash), Marta (Orlando Pride), Monica (Orlando), Poliana (Orlando), Thaisa (Sky Blue FC), Aedo (Washington), Theresa Nielsen (Seattle Reign FC), Jodie Taylor (Seattle), Rachel Daly (Houston), Gunnhildur Jonsdottir (Portland Thorns FC), Denise O'Sullivan (North Carolina), Nahomi Kawasumi (Seattle), Rumi Utsugi (Seattle), Francisca Ordega (Washington), Elise Thorsnes (Utah Royals FC), Rachel Corsie (Utah), and Ana-Maria Crnogorcevic (Portland).[75]

Major League Soccer- the men's soccer league in the US- had twenty-three teams across the country for the 2018 season while the NWSL had nine. During the first season of the women's league; teams were located in Boston, MA; Rochester, NY; Piscataway, NJ; Washington DC; Chicago, IL; Kansas City, KS; Seattle, WA; and Portland, OR. In 2018, teams had shuffled a bit since then with Portland, Seattle, Chicago, New Jersey, and Washington holding the only remaining original teams. Additional teams as of 2018 rested in Cary, NC; Orlando, FL; Houston, TX; and Salt Lake City, UT.

The Seattle Reign held a powerful role in their host city. During their inaugural season, the team played outside of the city in nearby Tukwila at Starfire Stadium before moving to Memorial Stadium in 2014 where the team played until 2019. Memorial Stadium rests in the center of Seattle directly under the Space Needle. The Reign leased the seventy-year old stadium from the Seattle Public Schools, and- in 2018- the Reign announced they would be partnering with the City of Seattle to renovate the stadium as part of a city-wide renovation program (including renovating Key Arena where the city's WNBA team plays).[76]

The few complaints I heard from Reign fans while attending games were always only about the stadium in which the team played. Bathrooms appear to have not been renovated since the stadium's

---

[74] Purdy. 2018.
[75] Purdy. 2018.
[76] Cristobal. 2018.

build in the 1940's. Seating in the arena consisted of cement terraces with hard plastic chairs. Most fans brought their own cushions to sit on. The general geography of the arena consisted of two tunnels- south and north of the field. Each tunnel had entrances to seating- also only north and south- on the sides of the field (meaning there were no seats behind goals). While Memorial Stadium claims a roughly 12,000 seat capacity, the team closes off sections of the stadium to limit seating to about half that number.

Limiting seating to about six thousand fans worked for Seattle though. From the games I went to in 2018, the average crowd size was about five thousand- meaning five out of every six available seats were filled. While watching on television- that looks like the stadium is full enough to make viewers think they should consider going to live games, but just empty enough to show there are still tickets available. Alternatively, some NWSL teams partner with MLS teams (such as the Orlando Pride and the Houston Dash) and use their partner's stadium without the fan base to fill seats in the immense stadiums. While watching on television, games appear empty of fans and do not attract potential ticket sales.

This concept is by no means unique either. Stadiums across sports are downsizing to increase ticket sales. The University of Richmond in Virginia downsized their Robins Center from a nine thousand seat capacity to roughly seven thousand. In response, ticket sales increased, and the quality of fan experience improved. Stanford University renovated their football stadium to decrease seating capacity from eighty-five thousand to fifty thousand by replacing bench seating with higher quality seats. After downsizing, the stadium sold out nearly every game over the next two years.[77]

The Reign played their second game of the season on my birthday on 15 April (Hey everyone over at the Reign- feel free to send me birthday presents!) in New Jersey. Reign starting players included Megan Rapinoe, Jodie Taylor, Jasmyne Spencer, Allie Long, Beverly Yanez, Jess Fishlock, Christen Westphal, Lauren Barnes, Megan Oyster, Theresa Nielsen, and Michelle Betos. The weather in Piscataway was cold and rainy to dramatically oversimplify it. Few fans braved the cold conditions for the second hypothermic game in a row for the Reign's 2018 season.

---

[77] Steinbach. 2015.

During the first half, Megan Rapinoe scored at the 6th minute mark off a penalty kick. In the freezing temperatures, the Reign focused on controlling the ball on offense to prevent Sky Blue players from capturing the ball. Wind arrived after the 25th minute mark with gusts at sixteen miles per hour. During the second half of the game; temperatures dropped, and the rain became heavier. The camera crew worked hard to keep equipment clear for those watching from home.

On the field, players from both teams scrambled in the slippery conditions with several players needing assistance off the field. Betos made several saves throughout the second half with help from the Seattle defense. At the 86th minute, Spencer took a penalty kick for the Reign ending with the Sky Blue goalkeeper saving the ball. The game ended with a 1-0 win for Seattle. The frozen Reign players returned to Seattle with their second win in two games for the season.

Reign players were no strangers to their host city of Seattle. From the hastati free agents and rookies to the triarii allocated players, Seattle Reign FC athletes often interact with the people and places of the city. Perhaps the most creative display of team-city interactions came in 2017 when then-goalkeeper Haley Kopmeyer took teammates to different areas of the city (including a coffee shop each time) to showcase Seattle and learn more about her teammates in a YouTube series called "Stops with Kop." Seattle tourism according to Haley Kopmeyer can best be summarized with her series.

According to Stops with Kop, the best places to visit in Seattle are seeing the nature of West Seattle, riding a bike through the downtown area, exploring the many thrift stores, visiting the Seattle Aquarium, heading to the Unicorn (a bar that I can- with experience- say is excellent), taking hip-hop dance lessons at the Nest, and boating on one of Seattle's many lakes- plus getting coffee at one of the thousands of coffee shops in the city.

Reporters often end interviews with Reign players by asking about the athletes' favorite things to do in the city. One of Lauren Barnes' favorite activities is exploring the many farmer's markets in Seattle and tasting the seasonal foods the state of Washington has to offer. She also loves to go hiking, practice yoga, and explore the lakes and ocean around the city.[78] (Hey Seattle Tourism Bureau, want to sponsor my next book?)

The third week of NWSL games saw Ashlyn Harris (Orlando Pride) earn the Save of the Week award. McCall Zerboni (North Carolina Courage) won Player of the Week, and Lindsey Horan (Portland Thorns FC) won the Goal of the Week. Each team in 2018 was scheduled to play an average of one game per week with games typically on the weekends (Friday through Sunday). Occasional Wednesday games allowed two teams per week to take the weekend off (hence the Reign's lack of a week two game).

That meant the Reign would have to follow their free third week in the season with two games in week four. (Two free weeks instead of one followed the Reign's first game due to the Boston Breaker's sudden fold just before the start of the season). The first of these two week four games came on 18 April against the North Carolina Courage. Seattle's starters were Jodie Taylor, Kiersten Dallstream, Morgan Andrews, Beverly Yanez, Jess Fishlock, Allie Long, Christen Westphal, Yael Averbuch, Megan Oyster, Theresa Nielsen, and Michelle Betos. For the first time in the season, the Reign were able to play a game in warm, sunny weather.

During the first half of the match, the Courage played an intense offensive game. The Reign could barely hold the ball and were slow to transition from defense to offense. Betos made saves for Seattle at the 17th, 18th, and 20th minutes. Several shots on goal came from both teams, but the defensive players for both the Reign and Courage played strong to keep the score 0-0 going into the half. During the second half, referees failed to give penalties for the several fouls Courage players inflicted on Seattle's Allie Long. Both teams continued to take several shots before Jessica McDonald scored for the Courage in the 71st minute. More shots ensued, but the game ended with a 0-1 loss for the Reign.

Elsewhere in the league, the Portland Thorns defeated the Orlando Pride 2-1. Week four awards went to Aubrey Bledsoe (Washington Spirit) for Save of the Week, Merritt Mathias (North Carolina Courage) for Goal of the Week, and Sofia Huerta (Chicago Red Stars) for Player of the Week. Ten days after their second week four game, the Reign entered week five with a game in Orlando.

---

[78] Nuzest. 2018.

Seattle started the game with Beverly Yanez, Jodie Taylor, Nahomi Kawasumi, Rumi Utsugi, Allie Long, Jess Fishlock, Steph Catley, Kristen McNabb, Megan Oyster, Christen Westphal, and Michelle Betos. During the first half, Orlando was disorganized on offense- giving the Seattle midfield time to prepare. Shots at the 11th and 12th minutes ended with Seattle saves from both defenders and goalkeeper Michelle Betos. Seattle counter-attacked with shots at the 21st, 22nd, 29th, and 31st minutes; but the Orlando defense held.

Finally, Allie Long scored for Seattle at the 33rd minute with an assist from Megan Oyster off a set piece just outside of the box. Skirmishes followed for the remainder of the match before the two teams entered the half. During the second half, both teams entered the game strong. Marta scored for Orlando off a set piece in the 61st minute. Shots came from both teams throughout the second half, but the game ended in a 1-1 draw.

Following week five games, several NWSL players entered the injured player roster- including Megan Rapinoe of the Seattle Reign. Elsewhere in the league, the North Carolina Courage defeated the Houston Dash 1-0, the Washington Spirit tied with the Chicago Red Stars 1-1, the Utah Royals tied with the Portland Thorns 1-1, and the Orlando Pride defeated the Chicago Red Stars 2-0 in a Wednesday game. The week five Save of the Week went to Aubrey Bledsoe (Washington Spirit), McCall Zerboni (North Carolina Courage) earned Player of the Week, and Tobin Heath (Portland Thorns FC) earned the Goal of the Week. Sofia Huerta (Chicago) earned the April Player of the Month.

The April Team of the Month consisted of goalkeeper Aubrey Bledsoe (Washington Spirit). Defenders included Rebecca Sonnett (Portland Thorns FC), Becky Sauerbrunn (Utah Royals FC), Estelle Johnson (Washington), and Jaelene Hinkle (North Carolina Courage). Midfielders included McCall Zerboni (North Carolina), Crystal Dunn (North Carolina), and Sofia Huerta (Houston Dash). Forwards included Mallory Pugh (Washington), Jessica McDonald (North Carolina), and Francisca Ordega (Washington).[79]

"Break a Sweat" Becky G

---

[79] Purdy. 2018.

People often think about the term "nationalism" as describing a person's loyalty to their federal government- but nationalism can be applied to loyalty to any organized people. For example, people from Texas have a deep sense of nationalism for their state. (I can't blame them. Texas has great BBQ, a historic Tejano culture, and excellent country-western music.) Nationalism within women's soccer is a bit more complex however.

Athletes on rosters for national teams across the world (such as Rumi Utsugi of Japan or Megan Rapinoe of the US) are required to put their national team ahead of their club in priority. If an athlete is called up to play in an international game, that player leaves their club temporarily to represent their country. In World Cup and Summer Olympic years, the NWSL suspends play temporarily for these two tournaments while their "triarii" athletes are away for games. In World Cup qualifying years, soccer matches go on in the uninterrupted schedule of the NWSL- with a clause.

In the army of the Roman Republic, a supplemental soldier type called "rorarii" served to fill the space of absent triarii in battle.[80] Because national team players would need to leave the league often in 2018 to compete in World Cup qualifying matches- and because the league would not suspend play during these events- the NWSL allotted each team a number of "national team replacement players" which would allow each team to have more athletes than the usual roster limit with the additional players serving as replacements for the "triarii of the NWSL" when away from league play. The Seattle Reign signed only one National Team Replacement player in 2018- Jaycie Johnson.[81]

Apart from national team players, athletes in the NWSL hold their loyalty to league and club- though the balance between these two can sometimes tip toward one more than the other. During the 2017/18 offseason, the Chicago Red Stars traded USWNT player Christen Press to the Houston Dash- a move that did not impress the athlete. Instead of playing for the Dash, Press left the NWSL entirely and returned to the Swedish league.[82]

---

[80] Erdkamp. 2011.
[81] Seattle Reign FC. 2018.
[82] Klein. 2018.

I first interpreted this as a result of loyalty to the Chicago club- since the athlete would rather leave the league entirely than play for any other team. My outlook changed however when news arrived that the Utah Royals had acquired the rights to Christen Press from the Houston Dash should she ever decide to return to the NWSL. Almost immediately, Press announced she was leaving Sweden to return to the NWSL to play on the new Utah team.[83]

The NWSL's clearest club-level nationalism however is best summarized by what may be the greatest rivalry in women's soccer anywhere in the world- the Cascadia Clash. The geographical region of Cascadia stretches along the Cascade Mountains from Northern California to Southern British Columbia with the cities of Portland and Seattle forming the largest cities on the US side of the region. The Cascadia Clash has long described the rivalry between these two cities' men's soccer teams, so when women's teams came to the region; the rivalry spilled over into the NWSL.

For the 2018 season, the Seattle Reign and Portland Thorns would have their first clash in their first games of May. Seattle started the game with Beverly Yanez, Jodie Taylor, Nahomi Kawasumi, Rumi Utsugi, Allie Long, Jess Fishlock, Steph Catley, Kristen McNabb, Megan Oyster, Christen Westphal, and Michelle Betos. The latter of which was an interesting choice. After playing for the Reign in the 2013 season, Betos served as goalkeeper for the Portland team for the 2014, 2015, and 2016 seasons before returning to the Reign in 2018. (Betos had played in the Norwegian league for the 2017 season.)

During the first half of the game, Michelle Betos found herself hard at work making saves at the 9th minute to start the match. The Thorns goalkeeper Britt Eckerstrom found herself at work making a save at the 22nd minute. Soon after, Betos made another save with help from Christen Westphal. At the 36th minute, Beverly Yanez scored for Seattle with an assist from Nahomi Kawasumi's corner kick. Before the half, Betos made another important save. In the second half, the Reign were hard at work again with Betos making a save at the 55th minute and Megan Oyster made a save at the 59th minute.

---

[83] Lee. 2018.

Intense defense could not save the Seattle team as Rebecca Sonnett scored for Portland in the 61st minute. Soon after however, Jodie Taylor scored for Seattle with a penalty kick, but Lindsey Horan quickly followed it up with a goal for Portland in the 70th minute. Rumi Utsugi counter attacked and scored for Seattle five minutes later. The Reign switched to defense and held off three more Portland attempts at goals before the game ended in a 3-2 win for Seattle. (That's donut number one Doc Ox needs to eat for those counting.)

The cities of Portland and Seattle themselves may perfectly represent the reason for the Cascadia Clash within the NWSL. Any visitor to the city of Portland would quickly understand the city by no means attempts to hide its "weird" side. From the vacuum museum to the emporium of strange things, Portland embraces its alternative culture. There are boxcar races, tiny parks, and peculiar donuts.[84] Alternatively, Seattle seems to hide its "weird" side. People that used to play grunge music in their garage back in high school now wear suits and ties on their way to tech jobs. Strange locations (like the haunted soda machine) are disappearing, and large office buildings are taking over the city.

Portland Thorns undoubtedly have the greatest fan support in the NWSL. The average attendance for a 2017 Thorns match was about 16,500 per home game. The second highest attendance for a team went to the Orlando Pride with half that number (about 8300). The Thorns benefit from a number of factors in their ticket sales success. The team partners with the MLS team, including using their stadium and governing board. There's a long history of soccer in Portland, especially within the Thorns team itself with a 2013 NWSL championship win. The greatest factor in the team's success stems from their fans known as the Rose City Riveteers- members of which never fail to hold back their enthusiasm for the team.[85]

The Seattle Reign had an average attendance in 2017 of about 3700 tickets sold per home game. Seattle too has a long history of soccer, but the Reign do not partner with the city's MLS team. In a 2017 survey, researchers found Reign fans often do not attend games due to a number of reasons- such as the overabundance

---

[84] Wulff. 2017.
[85] Torres. 2017.

of available activities in the city and a preference for attending men's soccer games. Fans often complain about Memorial Stadium, but ultimately the biggest issue is awareness. While Thorns jerseys can be found throughout Portland on any given day, many citizens of Seattle don't even know they have a professional women's soccer team.[86]

The sixth week in the NWSL season ended with Alyssa Naeher (Chicago Red Stars) earning Player of the Week and Save of the Week, and Diana Matheson (Utah Royals FC) earning Goal of the Week. On 10 May, I hopped on another plane and headed back to Seattle for my second research trip for the season. I arrived in town to catch a 12 May game between the Seattle Reign and Sky Blue FC. The Reign would play another game in warm, sunny weather. Before the start of the game, I spoke with several fans around me about what drew them to come to games.

One woman pointed out two children on the field involved in the opening ceremony. She told me her two kids had long wanted to be on the field during one of the ceremonies. During the conversation, I noticed most of the people attending the game were families. The Reign had a completely different fan base than a men's sports team. The Portland Thorns had the support of their city's MLS team fans, but that meant the same rowdy crowd for men's soccer came to the women's soccer games- a fan base that even the Rose City Rollers admit is not entirely appropriate for young attendees.

The Reign fans instead consisted of mostly families with young girls and boys wearing their favorite players' jerseys, rainbow flags waving everywhere, and fans booing referees far more commonly than opposing team players. One of those families overheard my conversation, and the dad turned around to join in. He explained his family was once a host family for the Seattle Reign.

In the first years of the league, teams in Seattle tackled the housing money shortage by bunking players with local families the way foreign exchange students stay with host families while in school in other countries. The father speaking to me explained his family hosted one of the Reign players until his son started going through puberty and decided he didn't want to subject professional athletes to his awkward son's "debonair" personality.

---

[86] Cristobal. 2017.

During the first half of the game, the Reign were quick to go on the attack with shots on goal at the 3rd and 5th minutes. Jodie Taylor scored shortly after as the Seattle attack continued. At the 15th minute, Sky Blue counter attacked, but the Seattle defense held. The Reign were quick to return to offense leading to Megan Rapinoe scoring for Seattle in the 39th minute. During the second half, referees remained mute during clear penalties.

Both teams grappled over the ball with Rapinoe scoring again at the 61st minute followed by Savannah McCaskill scoring for Sky Blue two minutes later. Several injuries occurred in the second half as a result of the referee's unwillingness to dish out penalties-forcing both teams to make several substitutions. (One fan near me shouted obscenities at the referee and nearly earned a forced withdrawal from the game.) At the 84th minute, Allie Long scored for Seattle before more injuries occurred. The game ended in a 4-1 victory for the Reign.

During my second trip to Seattle, I stayed with an old friend I made via couchsurfing in the Queen Anne neighborhood of the city. Queen Anne took me to an outdoor bar during my first night in Seattle where I would later discover through social media several Reign players frequented. The bar included large-scale beer pong. On the night following the Reign game, Queen Anne took me to a concert in the city. I worked off a harsh hangover the next morning ahead of my return flight to Alaska.

On my return journey to Sitka, I saw the updates from the week's matches. Houston and Portland tied 1-1 and tied Chicago 2-2, and Utah and Orlando tied 0-0. Orlando defeated Portland, and North Carolina defeated Washington. By the end of week seven, the NWSL teams were beginning to cement their positions on the leaderboard. From first to ninth, the teams ranked in the order of North Carolina, Seattle, Orlando, Portland, Chicago, Utah, Houston, Washington, and New Jersey.[87]

Week seven awards would end up going to Ashlyn Harris (Orlando Pride) for Save of the Week, Megan Rapinoe (Seattle Reign FC) for Player of the Week, and Christine Nairn (Orlando) for Goal of the Week. Megan Rapinoe is one of the few Seattle players to survive the two great purges of the Seattle Reign FC. After the

---

[87] NWSL. 2018.

Reign's disastrous 2013 season, the then general manager Laura Harvey expelled nearly the entire team to replace them with players that could take the Reign into the postseason.

Laura Harvey traded away Kristie Mewis and Michelle Betos in exchange for Sydney Leroux. Mariah Nogueira also joined the Reign after the 2013 season in exchange for Kaylyn Kyle. Seattle traded away Christine Nairn in exchange for rights to Kim Little, and the team waived several players to make space for future draft picks.[88] The drastic change paid off though, as the Seattle Reign finished the 2014 season in second place after losing in the postseason finals.

After another terrible season in 2017, the team followed their previous strategy by trading away or waiving the majority of their team. The Reign traded away Carson Pickett, Christine Nairn (whom the team recovered between 2015-17), and Haley Kopmeyer to acquire Steph Catley and Jasmyne Spencer. Carson Pickett entered the Reign as a 2016 college draft pick and Haley Kopmeyer had played for the Reign for all five previous seasons. Other players the Reign traded away included team favorites Katie Johnson, Diana Matheson, Rachel Corsie, and Merritt Mathias.[89]

The only Reign players in 2018 that had played every season with the team were Lauren Barnes, Jess Fishlock, Megan Rapinoe, and Kiersten "The Ghost" Dallstream. But perhaps the great purges- although painful at times to learn about as a fan of so many of the amazing athletes of the team- somehow worked. The Reign went from being one of the worst teams in the league in 2013 to being second in both 2014 and 2015 earning the NWSL Shield (an award that goes to the best defensive team in the league) two years in a row. The team saw many of their staples depart in 2016- explaining the rough 2017 season- and after a second extinction event in 2017, Seattle rebounded back to their golden age for the 2018 season.

On 19 May, the Reign prepared for their next game for week eight. Seattle started the game with Megan Rapinoe, Jodie Taylor, Nahomi Kawasumi, Rumi Utsugi, Allie Long, Jess Fishlock, Steph Catley, Lauren Barnes, Kristen McNabb, Alyssa Kleiner, and Lydia Williams. The Reign forced the Chicago Red Stars goalkeeper into the game early with shots on goal at the 7th and 17th minutes.

---

[88] Farley. 2013.
[89] Seattle Reign FC. 2018.

Chicago players counter-attacked in force however as a light rain set in. Throughout the first half, Reign players attempted to breach the Chicago defense; but Red Stars defenders held strong. In the last moments of the first half, Chicago took to offense, and Williams made several saves to keep Seattle in the game. During the second half, the ball raged back and forth with shots from both teams; but the game ended in a scoreless draw.

Elsewhere in the league, Portland defeated Washington 1-0, Utah defeated Houston 1-0, and North Carolina defeated New Jersey 2-1. Week eight awards would go to Katelyn Rowland (North Carolina Courage) for Save of the Week, Crystal Dunn (North Carolina) for Player of the Week, and Carli Lloyd (Sky Blue FC) for Goal of the Week. On 23 May, the Reign had another mid-week game- this time against the Houston Dash.

Seattle started the game with Beverly Yanez, Jodie Taylor, Nahomi Kawasumi, Elizabeth Addo, Rumi Utsugi, Allie Long, Steph Catley, Lauren Barnes, Kristen McNabb, Alyssa Kleiner, and Michelle Betos. The game opened with Houston taking to offense, but Michelle Betos made an early save for the Reign at the 7th minute. Seattle counter-attacked, earning two corner kicks at the 8th and 9th minutes, but finalizing an attack in the 13th minute gave Beverly Yanez a goal for Seattle off an assist from Jodie Taylor.

Seattle continued their offense by putting the Dash goalkeeper to work in the 18th, 23rd, and 26th minutes. Ten minutes later, Betos made a second save for Seattle to keep the Reign up by one going into the half. In the second half, Betos made several saves in the first twenty minutes before Kristie Mewis scored for Houston at the 68th minute. The ball raged back and forth between the teams and well into stoppage time (when a game extends beyond the 90th minute). In the last seconds of the game, Veronica Latsko scored for Houston to defeat Seattle 2-1.

On 26 May, the Reign had another game to play- this time against Sky Blue FC for their second match-up of the season. The Reign started the game with Megan Rapinoe, Jodie Taylor, Elizabeth Addo, Rumi Utsugi, Jess Fishlock, Allie Long, Christen Westphal, Lauren Barnes, Kristen McNabb, Theresa Nielsen, and Lydia Williams. The Reign took control of the ball early and held possession for the majority of the half, but could not sink any shots into the net. After a scoreless first half, the Reign returned to the pitch in full force. A Seattle goal finally came when Megan Rapinoe scored in the 65th minute. Several more shots on goal followed, but the game ended in only a 1-0 win for the Reign.

Elsewhere in the league, Washington defeated New Jersey 1-0, North Carolina defeated Orlando 4-3, Portland defeated Utah 2-0, Orlando defeated Chicago, and Houston defeated Washington. The Player of the Week award went to Rachel Daly (Houston Dash), with Sydney Leroux (Orlando Pride) earning Goal of the Week and Ashlyn Harris (Orlando) earning Save of the Week. The May Player of the Month award went to Rachel Daly (Houston).

The May Team of the Month consisted of goalkeeper Abby Smith (Utah Royals FC). Defenders included Steph Catley (Seattle Reign FC), Abby Erceg (North Carolina Courage), Ali Krieger (Orlando Pride), and Becky Sauerbrunn (Utah). Midfielders included Kristie Mewis (Houston Dash), Lindsey Horan (Portland Thorns FC), and McCall Zerboni (North Carolina). Forwards included Rachel Day (Houston), Christine Sinclair (Portland), and Crystal Dunn (North Carolina).[90]

"Star Maps" Aly & AJ

June began for the Reign with a match against the Orlando Pride on 3 June. Seattle started the game with Kiersten Dallstream, Jodie Taylor, Nahomi Kawasumi, Rumi Utsugi, Beverly Yanez, Jess Fishlock, Christen Westphal, Lauren Barnes, Kristen McNabb, Theresa Nielsen, and Lydia Williams. Three former Reign players would also be on the field- but for the Orlando team- Sydney Leroux, Carson Pickett, and Haley Kopmeyer.

During the first half of the game, Seattle went on the offense, but Orlando defensive players kept possession about equal. Reign players took several shots on goal, but could not penetrate their former goalkeeper Kopmeyer to score. After a scoreless first half, both teams returned from halftime to resume equal possession of the ball. Both teams took several shots on goal during the second half, but Orlando players managed to take the offensive. Seattle replied with hard defense, and the game ended in a scoreless draw.

The NWSL had designated June as pride month for the league- with representatives from each team serving as designated

---

[90] Balf. 2018.

allies of the LGBTQ community. These "Athlete Allies" would spend the month collecting money to donate towards the LGBTQ community in their host cities. Players also wore special uniforms with the rainbow flag printed on their jerseys.[91] Not all athletes agreed with the campaign however.

While I could discuss the dissenting athletes, I don't believe doing so would in a way help forward the message the league was communicating with their celebration of Pride Month, so instead I want to focus on those Athlete Allies and the teammates they support. Women's sports leagues across the US have felt under pressure to become more politically active than ever before- with a large emphasis on active participation in women's and LGBTQ rights campaigns. In 2017, the NWSL penned support for the Texas LGBTQ community in response to inhumane legislation that targeted transgender identifying persons with bathroom assignment laws.[92]

Seattle is one of the leading cities in the US for supporting their LGBTQ community. During Pride Month in 2018, four of Seattle's five professional sports teams held events for Pride Month to celebrate and support the city's LGBTQ community. The Mariners (men's baseball team), Storm (women's basketball team), Sounders (men's soccer team), and Reign all donated $5 for every ticket sold to the GSBA Scholarship Fund during their designated "Pride Games."[93]

On behalf of the NWSL, the Seattle Reign had one of the largest collections of Athlete Allies for the 2018 Pride Month. Seattle Reign representatives included Yael Averbuch, Morgan Andrews, Beverly Yanez, and Christen Westphal.[94] The Reign are one of the oldest NWSL teams to partner with the Athlete Ally program, and it is no surprise given Seattle's long history with their LGBTQ community.

When Arthur Denny began extracting natural resources from the modern-day Seattle area, a neighborhood of vice developed in what is today Pioneer Square. The "Tenderloin" as it was known

---

[91] Balf. 2018.
[92] LGBT Soccer. 2017.
[93] Seattle Gay Scene. 2018.
[94] Balf. 2018.

included gambling halls, brothels, boarding houses, and a sizable community of alternative sexual practitioners. A state law in 1893 outlawed homosexual sex, but officials in Seattle ignored the law during the height of the Klondike Gold Rush when the Tenderloin District began making serious money for the city.

When the gold rush slowed, the city resumed enforcing the anti-gay laws of the state in Seattle. During the 1930's an official LGBTQ community developed in the city when Seattle's industrial network expanded the city's population from about 3500 in 1880 to 365,500 in 1930. The Casino Pool Hall in Pioneer Square allowed same-sex dancing for the first time in the city (under the name Madame Peabody's School of Dance to disguise them from authorities).

After World War II, the number of gay bars in Seattle expanded in and outside of Pioneer Square. Drag shows became a central ritual in the Seattle LGBTQ community at this time- especially those held at the Garden of Allah. During the Lavender Scare of Cold War USA, Seattle gay bars often bribed police in the city to prevent raids like in San Francisco and New York City. After the police raid on Stonewall Inn in NYC however, the Seattle LGBTQ community began working towards officially ending the discriminatory state laws.[95]

During week ten of the 2018 NWSL season, Utah defeated New Jersey 2-1, Chicago defeated Washington 2-0, and North Carolina tied with Houston 1-1. Yuki Nagasato (Chicago Red Stars) earned Player of the Week, Katherine Reynolds (Portland Thorns FC) earned the Goal of the Week, and Haley Kopmeyer (Orlando Pride) earned the Save of the Week. Several international games included NWSL "triarii" that drew national team athletes away from the league for a two-week period.

Several NWSL players represented Canada during their 2-3 loss to Germany with Christine Sinclair (Portland Thorns FC) scoring for Team Canada. Yanara Aedo (Washington Spirit) represented Chile in their 4-0 win over Costa Rica. Theresa Nielsen (Seattle Reign FC) represented Denmark in their 5-1 win over Ukraine. Rachel Daly (Houston Dash) and Jodie Taylor (Seattle Reign FC) represented England in their 3-1 win over Russia.

---

[95] Aguirre & McKenna. 2016.

Gunnhildur Jonsdottir (Portland) represented Iceland in their 2-0 win over Slovenia. Denise O'Sullivan (North Carolina Courage) represented Ireland in their 2-0 loss to Norway- the latter of which included Elise Thorsnes (Utah Royals FC).

Nahomi Kawasumi and Rumi Utsugi (both Seattle Reign FC) played for Japan in the country's 3-1 win over New Zealand- the latter of which included Katie Bowen (Utah Royals), Rebekah Stott (Sky Blue FC), and Rosie White (Chicago Red Stars). Francisca Ordega (Washington Spirit) represented Nigeria in their 1-0 win over Gambia. Rachel Corsie (Utah) helped Scotland defeat Belarus 2-1.

Ana-Maria Crnogorcevic (Portland Thorns FC) helped Switzerland defeat Belarus 5-0. Jess Fishlock (Seattle) helped Wales win 1-0 over Bosnia and Herzegovina and 3-0 over Russia. The US won two games against China People's Republic with both games ending 1-0. Alex Morgan (Orlando Pride) scored in the first game and McCall Zerboni (North Carolina) scored in the second.[96]

Upon their return to the NWSL, the Reign's international players entered a match against the Washington Spirit on 16 June. Seattle started the match with Megan Rapinoe, Jodie Taylor, Beverly Yanez, Elizabeth Addo, Rumi Utsugi, Allie Long, Steph Catley, Lauren Barnes, Megan Oyster, Theresa Nielsen, and Lydia Williams. During the first half, Seattle assumed a strong offense, but Spirit defensive players prevented any goals.

Shots on goal came in numerous quantities from both teams, but the defenders and goalkeepers held the score at 0-0 going into the half. During the second half, the Spirit offense took control and made several shots on goal, but could not score before Seattle's counter-attack. Spirit defenders held the Reign back however- preventing Seattle from scoring. After an intense game, the two teams had to settle for a scoreless draw.

Elsewhere in the league, Chicago and Portland also tied with a score of 1-1. Orlando defeated New Jersey 3-2, and Utah defeated North Carolina 1-0 in North Carolina's first loss of the season. For the fortnight week 11/12; Britt Eckerstrom (Portland Thorns FC). earned the Save of the Week, Aubrey Bledsoe (Washington Spirit) earned the Player of the Week, and Brittany Ratcliffe (Utah Royals

---

[96] Purdy. 2018.

FC) earned the Goal of the Week. Elsewhere in Seattle sports, a different women's sports team was also rising from a terrible 2017 season towards success.

In 2017, Seattle's WNBA team- the Storm- finished the season in eighth place out of twelve teams. The Storm lost a single-game elimination in their attempt to enter the 2017 postseason. While the team had quality athletes, leadership could not hold the team together- especially after the loss of their head coach ahead of the playoffs.[97] During the 2018 season, the Storm were having their best season in almost a decade- and Reign players were watching.

Since the Reign joined Seattle's list of professional sports teams, Reign players developed a tradition of watching Storm games while on the road for their own matches in the NWSL and visiting home games while in Seattle. The partnership however between the teams went beyond viewership. In 2018, Seattle Storm player Sue Bird and Seattle Reign player Megan Rapinoe went public with their relationship and even appeared together in the 2018 ESPN Body Issue together as the first same-sex couple to appear in the magazine's body issue in the same photos.[98]

The majority of relationships in the NWSL remain private however. Regardless of orientation, public relationships can negatively affect a female athlete's career. US Olympic fencer Monica Aksamit spoke in March 2018 about how female athletes often need to keep their relationship status private because single female athletes get more followers on social media, and athletes with more social media followers get more sponsorships- meaning single female athletes get more sponsorships (via the transitive property). The more public a female athlete is with their dating life, the less social media followers they have.[99]

On a separate scale, single female athletes have to be careful about publicizing their dating lives to prevent stalkers. In 2016, a man who disguised himself as a utility meter attendant entered tennis player Petra Kvitova's apartment and attempted to rob the athlete under knife-point. The athlete managed to fight off the assailant, but

---

[97] Roberson. 2017.
[98] Vagianos. 2018.
[99] Aksamit. 2018.

not before sustaining a debilitating knife wound to her hand in the process.[100]

On 23 June, Seattle continued their month's schedule with a game against the North Carolina Courage. The Reign started the match with Megan Rapinoe, Jodie Taylor, Beverly Yanez, Elizabeth Addo, Rumi Utsugi, Allie Long, Steph Catley, Kristen McNabb, Megan Oyster, Alyssa Kleiner, and Lydia Williams. The first half began with a Courage offensive- with shots on goal at the 3rd, 7th, 14th, 15th, and 16th minutes.

Each shot of the barrage ended with Seattle properly defending the goal with Williams making several saves. A rapid Reign counter attack at the 18th minute ended with Megan Oyster scoring a goal off a corner kick from Megan Rapinoe. Lynn Williams returned the favor however by scoring for North Carolina at the 27th minute. The Courage continued their attacks, but Lydia Williams made each necessary save until the Reign could repost. Crystal Dunn regained the ball however and scored for the Courage at the 33rd minute.

The two teams returned from the half with more offensive plays. Merritt Mathias scored for North Carolina at the 47th minute to make it a 3-1 game. Courage players were luring Seattle into the offense against a superior, maneuverable defensive position as a means of stripping the ball and sending it to forward players. Lydia Williams had to make several more saves for Seattle before the game ended in a 1-3 loss for the Reign.

Elsewhere in the league, Portland defeated Houston 3-1, Chicago defeated Utah 2-0, and Orlando defeated Washington 1-0. Crystal Dunn (North Carolina Courage) earned the Player of the Week award. Alanna Kennedy (Orlando Pride) earned the Goal of the Week, and Ashlyn Harris (Orlando Pride) earned the Save of the Week. The Seattle Reign were slipping. After starting the 2018 season with strength, the Reign were ranked sixth in the league following their June loss to North Carolina.[101]

What sets the Seattle Reign apart from other athletic teams enduring a losing streak however is the team's grit. Fred Hutchison Cancer Research Center Board of Trustees member Leigh Morgan

---

[100] Rothenberg. 2016.
[101] NWSL. 2018.

describes "grit" as the passion and persistence of a person or persons in pursuing a goal- and goes further to detail her preference of grit as a character trait over raw, natural talent.[102] The character trait certainly describes each member of the 2018 Seattle Reign team, but grit also is increasingly defining women across more than sports teams.

Across the world, the definition of femininity is changing- and becoming increasingly post-modern. [I feel the need to note here that the definitions of words can certainly mean different things in different contexts. For the purposes of *this* book, the definitions of the terms "Modernism" and "Postmodernism" shall be described here. Modernism shall in this book define a singular definition or world-view while Postmodern shall describe a individualistic or diverse range of definitions for a term or world-view.]

Modern definitions of gender establish a uniform set of characteristics associated with masculinity and femininity- establishing a strict two-gender system. In opposition, Post-Modern definitions of gender allow each individual to identify with their preferred gender, or to establish an entirely unique gender identity. In the 21st Century, women can be described as feminine by wearing high heels en route to a formal dinner, or may be feminine by lacing up soccer cleats and heading into a game.

Ahead of the 2016 Rio Olympics, British track & field star Dina Asher Smith explained what femininity meant to her- defining it as strength, resilience, and perseverance.[103] These three character traits can be equally applied to men though, so what that means is that the very notion of gender as a divider in any given society- especially in sports- is out-dated.

This does not simply go beyond self-definitions either. Several examples in history exist of female athletes defeating male athletes in their respective sports. In 1975, Jackie Tonawanda knocked out Larry Rodania in a New York City boxing match. In 2003, Katie Hnida became the first woman to score points in an NCAA Division 1-A college football game as kicker for the University of New Mexico. In 1973, Billie Jean King defeated Bobby Riggs in the famous "Battle of the Sexes" tennis match.[104]

---

[102] Seatte Reign FC. 2018.
[103] Elle. 2016.

More recently, the top men and women in the surfing world traveled to Kelly Slater's artificial wave pool in Lemoore, California to put artificial wave technology to the test. While both sets of athletes were able to compete on equal waves with equal opportunity, the female surfers far surpassed their male counterparts in scores. In the top eighteen rides of the event, women set eleven scores. Two of the top three scores came from one woman (Stephanie Gilmore) whose four rides all made the top ten rankings.[105]

Perhaps then gender self-identity is as important as astrology and Harry Potter houses. In astrology, persons categorized by their birthday are given character traits that lead towards the individual furthering their self-identification with their societal-given astrological sign. [If you're wondering, I'm an Ares.] Gender identity today though may lean more towards Harry Potter houses.

To give context (in case any of this book's readers have no idea what or who Harry Potter is), author JK Rowling wrote a series of books centered around a main character named Harry Potter- a young boy going through wizardry school. In the series, a magical hat separates students at the boarding school into four "houses" based on character traits, but Rowling later revealed through the story that the hat ultimately assigns a house based on the student's preferred identity.

All athletes in the NWSL self-identify as women, but each athlete defines their femininity differently. Some keep their hair short, while others grow it long. Some dress in skirts and dresses outside of the pitch, while others prefer pants suits. Some are openly gay, and others keep their relationship status private. At the very end of all arguments, femininity is well-exemplified by the athletes of the NWSL as a changing term of self-definition.

An excellent metaphor for the dualistic relationship between societal definition and self-definition is soccer. Two teams attempt to define their own success and their opponent's. While a team can identify as champions, they must navigate through societal definitions for that title through winning games. For the Reign to truly define their quality, it would need to come with the struggle of

---

[104] Zemler. 2017.
[105] WSL. 2017.

competition within the NWSL- a competition that would continue in a 27 June Wednesday game against the Utah Royals FC.

The Reign began the game with Megan Rapinoe, Jodie Taylor, Nahomi Kawasumi, Morgan Andrews, Rumi Utsugi, Allie Long, Steph Catley, Kristen McNabb, Megan Oyster, Theresa Nielsen, and Michelle Betos. During the first half, Utah took to the attack with several shots on goal at the 3rd, 5th, 8th, 13th, and 16th minutes- with Betos making important saves at each shot.

Utah continued their attack with shots at the 18th, 23rd, and 24th minutes. Seattle finally took to the attack, but could not breach the Utah defense before ending the first half in a scoreless draw. In the second half, Seattle went on the offensive; but Royals players maintained possession of the ball. Both teams' players took several shots on goal, but to no avail. The game ended in another draw for the Reign.

Seattle desperately needed a win if they wanted to make the postseason. In the NWSL, only four teams compete beyond the regular season- meaning the top four teams at the end of regular season games enter the postseason (there are no competing conferences like in Major League Baseball). The Reign's last game in June would pit them against their long-time rivals- the Portland Thorns FC. On 30 June, the Reign began the game with Megan Rapinoe, Jodie Taylor, Elizabeth Addo, Beverly Yanez, Rumi Utsugi, Allie Long, Steph Catley, Lauren Barnes, Megan Oyster, Theresa Nielsen, and Lydia Williams.

This time, Seattle was quick to go on the attack with shots at the 9th, 10th, 17th, and 18th minutes. The attacks only increased- applying heavy pressure on the slowly crumbling Portland defense- but the first half ended without any goals. In the second half, several players fell from injury with Steph Catley walking off the field with a bloody nose. As players continued to drop from both sides, Seattle continued their attacks with Jodie Taylor scoring in the 89th minute off an assist from Megan Rapinoe. The Reign won the game 1-0 and kept themselves in contention for a postseason spot. (That's two donuts for Doc Ox.)

In fact, the Seattle Reign jumped all the way back to the number two spot on the league's standings with North Carolina holding at number one and Portland settling in fifth place.[106]

Elsewhere in week fourteen games, Houston defeated Orlando 2-1, Portland and New Jersey tied 1-1, North Carolina defeated Orlando 3-0, and Utah defeated New Jersey 3-1. Adriana Franch (Portland Thorns FC) earned both Player of the Week and Save of the Week while Kealia Ohai (Houston Dash) earned the Goal of the Week. Crystal Dunn (North Carolina Courage) earned the Player of the Month award for June.

The June Team of the month included Alyssa Naeher (Chicago Red Stars) as goalkeeper. Defenders included Rebecca Moros (Utah Royals FC), Becky Sauerbrunn (Utah), Abby Erceg (North Carolina Courage), and Merritt Mathias (North Carolina). Midfielders included Lindsey Horan (Portland Thorns FC), Yuki Nagasato (Chicago), and McCall Zerboni (North Carolina). Forwards included Kealia Ohai (Houston Dash), Christine Sinclair (Portland), and Crystal Dunn (North Carolina).[107]

"Summer Girl" HAIM

On 5 July, I packed my bags again for my third research trip to Seattle. After an airport brunch, two flights, and a quick light rail trip into the city center; I checked into my hostel in Seattle, met my hostel roommates, and got dinner. That night, I played a board game with fellow hostelers from Cleveland and Boston, spoke with a couple of Irishmen, then went to bed early.

I spent my Friday with a couchsurfer host from nearby Bellevue and his guest from Stuttgart. I impressed Bellevue with my knowledge of the city's haunted soda machine, so he took it upon himself to find locations in the city I had never been to before. (Four years of travel through Seattle has allowed me to knock a lot of destinations off the "things to see in Seattle" list.) Bellevue took Stuttgart and me to a rooftop garden with vehicles filled with plants and a great view of the Space Needle. After Bellevue left to go to work, Stuttgart and I got lunch under the needle before departing to explore the city.

While having lunch, Stuttgart and I talked about my travels. Stuttgart was fascinated by my desire to avoid wealthy desk jobs for [barely] a career of traveling the world. Stuttgart had just begun her

---

[106] NWSL. 2018.
[107] Purdy. 2018.

own adventure to travel the world after leaving her own desk job. My purpose for writing about women's sports was essentially the same reason why many athletes compete in the NWSL.

It is certainly not a well-paying job. As opposed to the NFL or the NBA, the NWSL is one of the lowest paying jobs in the US, and a woman soccer player would be financially better off quitting soccer and accepting a boring desk job somewhere (like tech jobs in Seattle). But those soccer players keep playing soccer for the same reason why I keep writing these books- because its what they enjoy.

I told Stuttgart, "I worry more that I might not enjoy a job than I might not make money."

When I returned to the hostel, I spoke with two young Swiss women in my hostel room about surfing- as one was intent on convincing me to give her my "Trestles" hat from the Swatch Pro. (I didn't give her the hat.) While at the hostel, I continued to feel I had in some way elevated through my experiences of travel into my own principe class. I tended to spend time with travelers in their late 20's and early 30's rather than the young "gap year" travelers. I spent the night with Bellevue and Stuttgart again, this time for dinner at a Greek pizza place before returning to the hostel to play cards with the Swiss women and a German man.

On Saturday, I was all about game day. I met up with a Brazilian volleyball player to introduce her to the Reign Top Pot donut and learned more about how it feels to watch the increasing number of Brazilian athletes in the NWSL. Sao Paulo was a huge fan of Marta (Orlando Pride) who consistently receives the FIFA Player of the Year award and who has represented Brazil in more World Cups than any player has represented any nation in any women's world cup.

After breakfast, I went to Memorial Stadium for the game. While in line, I spoke to fellow season ticket holders about the history of the team. They told me about the gap year between the second and third women's leagues when the Sounders Women was the highest level of women's soccer in the city. We also discussed the various trades the team made over the years and how intimately fans of the team learn to respect every player the team has had (like Carson Pickett, Haley Kopmeyer, and Merritt Mathias whom people in line all mentioned by name in the conversations).

I then headed for the beer garden at Memorial Stadium where I met a married couple that moved from North Carolina to Seattle for work. We talked about the Courage. (The two had moved with their children before North Carolina gained an NWSL team.) We talked about former Reign players and the teams they were now playing with, as well as future possible college draft picks and the strength of the University of Washington women's soccer team. After thirty minutes in the beer garden, I headed for my seat and prepared for the start of the game.

During the first half of the game, offensive plays fell roughly evenly among Seattle and Houston. Amber Brooks scored for Houston in the 12th minute, but the Reign managed to penetrate the Houston defense in the 38th minute when Jodie Taylor scored to tie the game. During the second half, Seattle dominated possession with several shots at the 47th and 48th minutes before Megan Rapinoe scored in the 56th minute. Injured players and substitutions ensued for Seattle before Houston took control of the ball midway through the half. A Reign counterattack came after Jasmyne Spencer entered the game in the 83rd minute. At the 85th minute, Allie Long scored for Seattle to make it a 3-1 game- the final score of the game.

Elsewhere in the league that week, North Carolina defeated Chicago 4-1, Portland defeated Utah 4-0, Chicago defeated New Jersey 3-1, and Orlando defeated Washington 2-1. Sam Kerr (Chicago Red Stars) earned the Player of the Week award, Marta (Orlando Pride) earned the Goal of the Week, and Adriana Franch (Portland Thorns FC) earned the Save of the Week. After the game, Bellevue and Stuttgart picked me up from my hostel.

Bellevue took me to another yet-unseen Seattle location- outdoor ping-pong tables. After a couple of beers at a local bar, the three of us went back to Bellevue's condo where I would stay for the remainder of my trip. The next day, I wanted to learn more about what drew Reign fans to Storm games- beyond the geographic allegiance. On Sunday, I bussed to Key Arena- also under the Space Needle- to watch my first live Storm game. It was electric.

I arrived during the second quarter to find a packed arena with a loud crown (more of a mob) cheering players and booing referees. (There was also "bottomless popcorn" which is popcorn with unlimited refills, and it is the greatest thing ever. Good job, Seattle Storm.) After the game, I bought a Storm hat and Storm socks because I was hooked. The game was incredible with the points going back and forth right into the final moments of the clock with Seattle taking the final lead just seconds before the end to give them the win.

After the game, Bellevue picked me up with a new couchsurfer from Stockholm. The three of us went to another yet-unseen location in Seattle- a forbidden beach where the ruins of a sea wall were crumbled into the beach below and covered in spray paint. After exploring the beach for a while, we climbed back up the tall cliff face (including using each other as human ladders to scale the cliff face), picked up Stuttgart, and got dinner. The next morning; we had brunch at one of Seattle's many lake-side beaches, dropped Stuttgart off at her hostel and Stockholm off in the city center, then returned to Bellevue's condo.

Actually, I feel the need to add details to our time at brunch. I was craving a good dessert and saw the brunch place had "molten lava cake." Now, where I come from, molten lava cake comes with a sparkler (like what's sold at firework stores), so I was torn between choosing the molten lava cake or the bread pudding. When the waitress came by, I told her I had a question, and the answer to my question would determine what I would be getting.

"What's your question?" the waitress asked nervously.

"With the molten lava cake," I spoke, "is there open flame involved?"

"No," the waitress answered, almost not believing I had just asked such a question.

I replied, "I'll be getting the bread pudding then."

Later that night, Bellevue and I picked up another new couchsurfer- this time a mountaineer from Colorado- and brought her to a third new location for me in Seattle. This was a top-floor restaurant in the tallest building in Seattle where only club members and their guests may enter. After appetizers, the three of us met up with Stockholm and a friend of hers from Croatia over much needed chicken and waffles that I not-so-subtly hinted towards Bellevue about wanting. In truth, Bellevue surprised me with this one. He told Colorado and I we were going to a "bar that serves food late" and upon arrival, we met the other two outside.

Bellevue pointed to the sign outside the door with the restaurant's menu and said, "Now, I want everyone to find something in the world that makes them as happy as Joe will be after reading this menu."

I curiously leaned in to read what the restaurant served, and my eyes immediately found the words "chicken" and "waffles." I'm fairly certain at least one tear rolled down my cheek. Another day of similar situations followed before the Wednesday game day for the Reign brought me back into downtown Seattle. Before the game, I entered the stadium's beer garden to speak with staff and fans drinking local beers ahead of the match. The stadium was packed for the game with nearly every seat sold- not surprising since the Reign's longtime coach was now coaching for Utah, and many of the names on Reign fan's jerseys now listed players on the Royals roster.

During the first half, Seattle and Utah held roughly equal possession of the ball, and offensive plays raged from both sides. Lydia Williams made an important save at the 23rd minute, and Utah's goalkeeper saved at the 43rd. The first half ended in a scoreless tie with both teams in need of a win. In the second half, Megan Rapinoe scored an early goal at the 53rd minute for Seattle before referees began working hard to keep up with penalties for the remainder of the game.

At the 66th minute, Rachel Corsie earned a Yellow Card for a downed Seattle player. At the 71st minute, three athletes (two Reign and one Royals) went down on a triple collision. The remainder of the game was defined more by subbing out injured players than by offensive plays- and from both teams. Utah made subs at the 76th, 84th, and 90th minutes; and Seattle made subs at the 87th and 91st minutes- before the game ended in a 1-0 win for the Reign.

On Thursday, I returned to Alaska to begin preparations for my final research trip for the book. The Seattle Reign were also preparing for the final weeks of the season. From Wednesday's match against Utah and onward, every single game would have to count as the team attempted to enter the postseason. Apart from the obvious psychological pressure to succeed, there is also a financial pressure on the league's teams. The best example of why can actually be understood through the metaphor of superhero movies.

When it comes to superheroes, there are dozens of male characters the average non-comic book reading person knows by name; Batman, Spiderman, Superman. But while there are plenty of female characters in comic books, few people know who they are except for comic book readers. So when the Wonder Woman movie premiered in movie theaters in 2017, it had to be perfect. Anything less than a box-office smash would have meant no more female superhero movies.

Alternatively, there can be terrible male superhero movies (Spiderman 3, Batman and Robin, Superman Returns) and those characters can continue to get more movies. This double standard spills over into sports. If a men's soccer team ends a season in last place in their league, the team continues to live on into the next season. When a women's soccer team finishes a season in last place- as evident in the NWSL- the team was likely to either move or dissolve entirely.

Women's sports leagues then are comparable to reality television shows like the Bachelor or Survivor where contestants are slowly eliminated over the course of the show. The problem is that none of the athletes in the NWSL ever consented to *that* competition. In the NWSL, the team with the biggest losing streak is not necessarily the team removed from the league. Instead, it is typically the team that brings in the least overall capital for the league.

For example, even if a team wins the NWSL Championships; if that team sells few tickets throughout the season, sells few jerseys, and spends too much money on supporting athletes in housing and training services; that team will likely be removed from the league. From an economic point of view, that makes sense- a team that is costing the league money rather that making the league money should be removed as a means of keeping the league financially profitable. The problem is what that means for the athletes on the cut team.

One of the biggest money makers for the league is jersey sales. Because there are few teams in the league, fans typically have to watch games either on television or online- so viewership brings in only a small source of revenue for the league. Alternatively, jersey sales are high because of two probable reasons. The first is that few women's national teams sell their women's team jerseys with player names on the back.

(USA Soccer only began selling custom jerseys in 2018 for their USWNT players, and good luck finding a Welsh National Team apparel store for a Jess Fishlock jersey). The second major reason is that because travel to a live game is difficult, many parents buy their child's favorite player jersey for holiday and birthday presents rather than game tickets.

Choosing a jersey to buy comes down to design. Oftentimes, fans of women's soccer have favorite players on multiple teams (either because they are more likely to follow a national team, or because their favorite players over the years have been traded to other teams). Having the best designed jersey in the NWSL can drastically improve jersey sales.

In 2015, the Seattle Reign earned the top vote for best jersey of the season. The home jersey was a short-sleeved shirt divided into three vertical sections with black in the center and true blue on the flanks. The away jersey featured purple from the chest down, and florescent green above and entirely covering the back half of the shirt. The goalkeeper jersey was a long-sleeved shirt of ultra-violet with green bands at the elbow.[108]

It is no surprise then that from 2014-2017, the Seattle Reign were ranked among the top four teams in both revenue and expenses- the strongest in revenue for a team unsupported by a MLS team. When it comes to expenses, the Reign owners consistently report their commitment to investing club capital in providing quality training and health services for the players and in discovering new ways to expand their fan base. Owner Bill Predmore went further to report that for a sports league less than ten years old, profitability is an "elusive goal," and that the league and its teams should instead focus on growing revenue and increasing the quality of competition of the teams.[109]

An NWSL team's revenue is not always dependent on the league or sales either. Strong partnerships with sponsors define the league's teams- evident directly from the team jerseys. Apart from the importance of design in selling jerseys to fans, NWSL teams also feature the team's main sponsor in big letters on the center of their uniforms. These main sponsors are often referred to as "shirt sponsors" because they are the organization that gets their name on the team's jerseys.

---

[108] Rantz. 2015.
[109] Cristobal. 2017.

From 2013-2016, Moda Health held the "shirt sponsor" title with the Seattle Reign. In 2016 however, the Reign's jersey received an upgrade when Microsoft began partnering with the team as an effort to become the defacto shirt sponsor for every professional sports team in Seattle. In doing so, Microsoft made the Seattle Reign jersey the highest-profile jersey in the league through the sponsorship. Apart from financial assistance, Microsoft also provided athletic training software for the team.[110]

Partnerships and sponsorships reach far beyond the jersey designs. Most teams in the league partner with bars near their stadiums and host cities for away-game celebrations and post-game meet-and-greets with athletes. Local university hospitals often partner with teams to provide medical support and rehabilitation services for injured players. Financial service providers, corporate partners, coffee shops and restaurants, and local radio stations all partner with teams to provide financial aid and advertising for the teams.

As of 2018, "Premier Partners" (major financial sponsors just shy of earning the coveted spot on the jersey) for the Reign included Avanade, UW Medicine, BECU, and Carter Subaru. (Carter Subaru stands out as a partner because every time a Reign FC goalkeeper makes a true save or a save against a direct shot-on-goal, the car dealership plants a new tree in or around Seattle.)

Corporate sponsors included Thomas McKenny & Associates, Flow Fitness, Pepsi, Washington Athletic Club, Georgetown Brewing (which supplies the stadium beer garden), Seattle Divorce Services, Portage Bay, Atlantic Crossing (which hosts away-game celebrations), and Top Pot. Performance partners included The Grinning Yogi, Vida Integrated Health, Nuzest, Ivy Bjornson, and Admiral Bird. Media Partners included 950amKJR, C89.5fm, KOMO ABC 4, Power 93.3, Printing Control, The Seattle Times, Seattle Refined, RRD, and Intersection.[111]

On 13 July, the Reign would play their second game for week sixteen- this time against Chicago. Seattle started the game with Megan Rapinoe, Jodie Taylor, Nahomi Kawasumi, Jess Fishlock, Beverly Yanez, Allie Long, Steph Catley, Lauren Barnes,

---

[110] Soper. 2016.
[111] ReignFC.com. 2018.

Megan Oyster, Theresa Nielsen, and Michelle Betos. Reign players took an early offense with shots at the 13th, 15th, and 21st minutes; but Chicago quickly stripped the ball and went heavy on the attack. Chicago shots dominated the remainder of the first half with Seattle players making key saves to keep the game scoreless going into the second half.

During halftime, news came in that a Chicago player (Arin Gilliland) carried off the field by stretcher at the 35th minute had been evacuated to a hospital for treatment. During the second half, both teams equally pounded each other with offensive plays- even the fans in Chicago took to the attack when they booed every time Megan Rapinoe even touched the ball. Injuries on both teams forced substitutions (with referees handing out almost no penalties or cards) until the 87th minute with Sam Kerr scored for the Red Stars. The game ended in a 0-1 loss for the Reign.

Elsewhere in the league in week sixteen; North Carolina defeated Washington 2-0, Houston defeated Orlando 3-1, North Carolina defeated New Jersey 4-0, Orlando defeated Utah 2-1, and Portland defeated Houston 3-1. Lynn Williams (North Carolina Courage) won the Player of the Week award, Kristen Edmonds (Orlando Pride) earned the Goal of the Week, and Rachel Corsie (Utah Royals) earned the Save of the Week. Two days after the Reign-Red Stars game, the NWSL provided an update on Arin Gilliland's injury to report the league had taken precautions to ensure the safety of the player with fears of spinal damage, but the athlete had sustained no major injuries and left the hospital soon after her arrival.[112]

Injuries were becoming an increasing issue in the league. Referees were allowing unnecessary roughness- leading towards serious injuries during games and increasing animosity between fans and officials as well as athletes on opposing teams. Two major athlete suspensions came in the 2018 regular season with Meghan Klingenberg (Portland Thorns FC) and Diana Matheson (Utah Royals FC).

Meghan Klingenberg received a one-game suspension and a fine (of an undisclosed amount) after the Portland Thorns FC defender kicked Seattle Reign FC midfielder Allie Long during a 30

---

[112] Purdy. 2018.

June game. After Allie Long kicked the ball away during their duel, Klingenberg intentionally kicked Long in the knee. Both game referees refused to hand out any penalty for the clear foul (which would have been a red card violation- an instant one-game suspension). Instead, Klingenberg finished the game and the league head office had to retroactively deliver the penalty.[113]

Referees and coaches in the NWSL were reaching violent conflict in 2018 as well. The first referee-delivered red card came half-way through the 2018 season in a game between the Orlando Pride and the Houston Dash. Before the game, several violent encounters between players were rapidly increasing in the league's games. A week after Meghan Klingenberg received her suspension, another Thorns player became violent in a game against the Utah Royals when Margaret Purce slide-tackled Utah midfielder Diana Matheson with unnecessary aggression. Diana Matheson received a suspension for a similar maneuver in the following week's game.[114]

There are obvious inconsistencies in referee calls in the NWSL, and there may be a pattern. Socio-cultural anthropologist Ali Kenner described the anthropology of "necessary evils" with a story about the allowance of hazardous exposure to scrap yards in Somerset, England. In 2016, scrap yards in Somerset openly violated basic safety codes without repercussion from local authorities because the scrap yards provided a necessary service to the community, and no official wanted to be responsible for undermining a necessary service. In response; the scrap yards were directly responsible for creating toxic waste in the community, causing bushfires, and poisoning local water sources.[115]

There is a vast difference between the wealthiest and least wealthy clubs in the NWSL; and because clubs generate revenue for the league, some clubs can end up having a larger impact in league decisions than others. In order to maintain allegiance from its more powerful clubs, the NWSL and its officials are often pressured to cater to the demands of its wealthier teams. To return to the "kingdom" analogy, the NWSL is curving in a similar direction that

---

[113] Goldberg. 2018.
[114] Kassouf. 2018.
[115] Kenner. 2017.

often led Medieval kingdoms towards power shifts between their absolute monarchs and their increasingly powerful aristocrats.

The English Civil War is an excellent example of this. With an expanded legislature including lords from England, Wales, Scotland, and Ireland; King Charles I found himself needing to support an expanded population across several territories. When the king chose to spend resources on preventing an Irish insurrection, the English aristocrats overthrew the king and replaced the government with one that favored their interests.[116]

The NWSL team owners work as the league's metaphorical vassals; and with absent strong leadership (an empty League Commissioner position), team owners of the most profitable teams are gaining increasing authority over league decisions with less powerful league owners rapidly losing power. The result is an imbalance in power among persons with equal titles and is a dangerous sign of possible ruptures to come in the NWSL.

Team power can effectively be measured in stadium sizes and ticket sales among the teams. Teams with the most number of loyal fans are the least likely to be cut from the league- the "necessary" teams in keeping the league in business. In 2017, the average NWSL game sold 6600 tickets. Only the Portland Thorns FC with 17,650 tickets sold per game sold more tickets per game than the average. (Seattle Reign FC sold an average of 4000 tickets per game in 2017.)[117] Whether officially or unofficially, the NWSL definitely plays favorites with their Portland team. Early in 2018, the league announced the city would host the NWSL Championship game due to the size of the team's arena.

Also in 2018, the league overturned a suspension on Portland coach Mark Parsons during the team's season opener in North Carolina. In the original decision, game officials delivered a two-game suspension and an undisclosed fine to the Thorns head coach following a verbally violent outburst against a referee.[118] During the [spoiler alert] televised 2018 semifinal match between Portland and Seattle, viewers could clearly see Parson berating referees after an

---

[116] History.com. 2018.
[117] Soccer Stadium Digest. 2017.
[118] Goldberg. 2018.

"offside" call overturned a goal. The coach received no penalty from either referees or the league.

This unbalanced allowance of behavior does not only follow financial power either. In women's sports across the world, female athletes understand the power dynamic in conversations with referees well. During the 2018 US Open of Tennis, the head referee of the finals match between Serena Williams and Naomi Osaka penalized Williams for a thumbs up the athlete received from her coach (deemed "unlawful coaching"), and the athlete received further penalties for attempting to argue the original penalty.

In opposition, male tennis players famously berate referees without penalty in a perfect example of on-the-court sexism in tennis.[119] In 2018, there were three women head coaches in the NWSL; Vera Pauw (Houston Dash), Denise Reddy (Sky Blue FC), and Laura Harvey (Utah Royals FC)- none of which dared berate referees on Mark Parson's level.

On 21 June, the Reign played their sole week seventeen game. Seattle started their game against Orlando with Jasmyne Spencer, Jodie Taylor, Nahomi Kawasumi, Jess Fishlock, Beverly Yanez, Rumi Utsugi, Steph Catley, Lauren Barnes, Megan Oyster, Theresa Nielsen, and Lydia Williams. Both teams were playing without their allocated players- bringing the rorarii into the bench. Seattle dominated possession in the first half with shots at the 10th, 15th, 17th, 23rd, 37th, 39th, and 44th minutes with few Orlando plays in between.

A goal at the 21st minute from Toni Pressley gave Orlando an early lead however. In the second half, Seattle continued to dominate possession. Injuries defined the game though. Beverly Yanez had to sub out of the game in the first half. In the second, players went down at the 63rd, 89th and 90th minutes. A goal from Jodie Taylor off a Jess Fishlock assist at the 70th minute however gave Seattle the goal they needed to survive the game and end the match in a 1-1 draw.

Across the league, Jane Campbell (Houston Dash) earned the Player of the Week award, Toni Pressley (Orlando Pride) earned the Goal of the Week, and Rachel Corsie (Utah Royals FC) earned her second Save of the Week award in a row. Utah tied North Carolina

---

[119] McCausland & Silva. 2018.

in a scoreless draw, Portland defeated New Jersey 2-1, and Houston defeated Washington 1-0.

The following week provided a break for the league as several international tournaments took place. The two main events were the Tournament of Nations- pitting the USWNT against three other national teams and the North Carolina Courage club against three European clubs in the first ever tournament of its kind. Participating teams in the Tournament of Nations were the US, Australia, Japan, and Brazil. Participating clubs in the ICC tournament were the North Carolina Courage, Paris-Saint Germaine (France), Olympique Lyonnais (France), and Manchester City (England).

Two NWSL players represented Japan in the Tournament of Nations: Rumi Utsugi and Nahomi Kawasumi (both Seattle Reign FC). Ten NWSL players represented Australia: Ellie Carpenter, Cailtin Foord, and Hayley Raso (Portland Thorns FC); Alanna Kennedy and Emily van Egmond (Orlando Pride); Sam Kerr (Chicago Red Stars); and Kyah Simon (Houston Dash).[120] Seven NWSL athletes would represent Brazil: Marta, Camila, Monica, and Poliana (Orlando Pride); Thaisa (Sky Blue FC); Debhina (North Carolina Courage); and Andressinha (Portland).[121]

The US team had the largest selection of NWSL players. Goalkeepers included Adriana Franch (Portland Thorns FC), Ashlyn Harris (Orlando Pride), and Alyssa Naeher (Chicago Red Stars). Defenders included Abby Dahlkemper, Jaelene Hinkle, and Merritt Mathias (North Carolina Courage); Becky Sauerbrunn (Utah Royals FC); Casey Short (Chicago); and Rebecca Sonnett (Portland).

Defenders included Morgan Brian and Julie Ertz (Chicago); Lindsey Horan (Portland); Rose Lavelle (Washington Spirit); Carli Lloyd (Sky Blue FC); Sam Mewis and McCall Zerboni (North Carolina); and Allie Long (Seattle Reign FC). Forwards included Crystal Dunn (North Carolina); Tobin Heath (Portland); Alex Morgan (Orlando); Kealia Ohai (Houston Dash); Christen Press and Amy Rodriguez (Utah); and Megan Rapinoe (Seattle).[122]

---

[120] Purdy. 2018.
[121] Purdy. 2018.
[122] Purdy. 2018.

During the Tournament of Nations, the US defeated Japan 4-2 with NWSL player goals from Alex Morgan (Orlando Pride) and Megan Rapinoe (Seattle Reign FC); and Brazil defeated Japan 2-1 with NWSL goals from Marta (Orlando Pride). On the same day, the North Carolina Courage defeated Paris-Saint Germaine 2-1 with goals from Jessica McDonald and Darian Jenkins.

The US tied Australia 1-1 with an NWSL goal from Lindsey Horan (Portland Thorns FC). North Carolina Courage defeated Olympique Lyonnais 1-0 with a goal from Heather O'Reilly to win the first ICC event. In the Tournament of Nations, the US defeated Brazil 4-1 with NWSL goals from Rose Lavelle (Washington Spirit), Julie Ertz (Chicago Red Stars), and Alex Morgan (Orlando).

Elsewhere- in the Central American and Caribbean Games- Julie Johnson (Sky Blue FC) scored in Mexico's 3-1 victory over Costa Rica.[123] No weekly awards came for week eighteen games- since the only NWSL team that played during the week was North Carolina- and against non-league teams. The July Player of the Month award went to Lindsey Horan (Portland Thorns FC).

The July Team of the Month consisted of goalkeeper Adriana Franch (Portland). Defenders included Katie Naughton (Chicago Red Stars), Rachel Corsie (Utah Royals FC), Abby Erceg (North Carolina Courage), and Theresa Nielsen (Seattle Reign FC). Midfielders included Lindsey Horan (Portland), Yuki Nagasato (Houston Dash), and McCall Zerboni (North Carolina). Forwards included Sam Kerr (Chicago), Rachel Daly (Houston), and Megan Rapinoe (Seattle).[124]

The league standings at the end of July were beginning to coagulate. The four teams that would inevitably reach the postseason were all in the top four spots- North Carolina, Seattle, Portland, and Chicago. More dangerous however were the teams at the other end of the spectrum. Sky Blue FC had yet to win a game in the season and was sitting in eighth of nine spots.[125] That meant the team was at risk of disbanding. If New Jersey could not win a game before the end of the season, its chances of survival would drop dramatically.

---

[123] Purdy. 2018.
[124] Gabriel 2018.
[125] Purdy. 2018.

August would be the last opportunity for the team to prove to the league and its owners it was worth keeping around.

"Super Critical" The Ting Tings

On 3 August, I departed Sitka for my final research trip to Seattle. Bellevue hosted me again for this trip; so after several busses into- and then out of- Seattle, I unloaded my cargo at Bellevue's apartment and went to bed after a long travel time. Before Sunday's game, I spent my Saturday getting caught up on notes at the condo and met three couchsurfers from South Africa, Germany, and France. On Sunday, Bellevue and I introduced the three young women to Top Pot- especially their Reign FC themed donut.

Seattle is a city that seems like it was forced to mature to survive. The state that created Nirvana has become a state that produced Amazon and Microsoft. From afar, it can seem like the city has had to sacrifice who it used to be to become the city it is today- as evident from the dozens of new skyscrapers, upscale neighborhoods that seem to pop up every week, and new tech jobs attracting young college graduates from across the country. Even the city of Portland- known for its "keep it weird" philosophy- is changing. A city can only survive on decorative knot stores for so long before it needs large-scale industry to keep its economy growing.

Just like with cities, the NWSL needs financial growth to maintain itself. To do that, the NWSL's main goal has always been to increase its fan base- largely through media marketing and broadcasting. In 2013, Fox Sports aired six NWSL matches- three regular season and three postseason games. In 2014, that agreement switched to ESPN. For 2015-16, Fox Sports took back the deal and included a further four live-streamed games on the channel's mobile Fox Sports Go app.[126] All other games to date were broadcast either by the league or by individual teams on YouTube live.

For 2017-19, the league partnered with Lifetime for its televised games and the Go90 app for online broadcasts until the latter website folded midway through the 2018 season. One game per week would be broadcast on television (known as the "Lifetime Game of the Week") with all non-televised games broadcast on the

---

[126] Lauletta. 2016.

Go90 app. For international viewers, all games- even television broadcasts- would be available on the NWSL website. Even Lifetime departed their deal however- announcing they would not broadcast any 2019 games following the 2018 season.

The Seattle Reign began their 5 August game with a mostly defensive strategy. Washington Spirit players made several attempts at a goal with shots at the 2nd, 5th, and 9th minutes. Seattle wrestled control of the ball and controlled its possession for the remainder of the half. Finally- at the 44th minute- the Reign took the lead when Jasmyne Spencer scored a goal off an assist from Allie Long. After the half, Seattle again dominated possession. Jasmyne Spencer scored again at the 71st minute ahead of several more Seattle shots. With key saves from Lydia Williams, the Seattle Reign finished the game with a 2-0 win.

Elsewhere in the league, North Carolina defeated Portland 2-1, Orlando and New Jersey tied 2-2, and Utah defeated Houston 2-1. Lynn Williams (North Carolina Courage) earned the Player of the Week award, Katie Stengel (Utah Royals FC) earned the Goal of the Week, and Ashlyn Harris (Orlando Pride) earned the Save of the Week. The next day, I spent my Monday with Bellevue and his other guests on one of Seattle's many lakes in inflatable canoes- an activity not uncommon among the Seattle Reign.

The reason I know that is because of Instagram. The social media app allows athletes to connect with their fans with images and videos- and is a major source of scouting for sponsors looking to sign contracts with athletes. It is also a valuable resource for athletes who want to communicate with their fans without having to travel or meet people in person. Seattle Reign players often post images and videos of lake trips, hikes around Washington, and trips to local farmers markets.

Outside of social media, athletes from NWSL teams interact with their fans in organized in-person events. Most teams have designated areas at stadiums where fans can go after a game to take photos and receive autographs from their favorite players. Outside of games, teams host promotional events and celebrations. The Seattle Reign usually have two big events for season ticket holders- one before the start of a regular season and one after. Athletes individually or in small groups also travel around Seattle to take part in charity events.

In 2016, I actually accidentally found myself in one of these events. On my return journey to Alaska from my research venture on the role of women in rodeo history (which you can read all about in *Behind the Chute*), I lost my debit card somewhere in Colorado and had to go to the bank every morning to get cash from my account. During one morning's cash withdrawal in Seattle, the bank teller noticed my Wonder Woman coffee mug; and the two of us started talking about how I write books about women's sports.

A second woman standing next to me overheard our conversation and asked if I had heard of the Seattle Reign FC. (I was wearing a Reign FC jersey that day.) She told me she worked for a hospital across the street from the bank that was hosting a mural-painting event for the cancer ward, and that some of the Seattle Reign players would be there to help. The woman told me to come by if I wanted to meet any of the players, so of course I did.

I spent two hours next to Nahomi Kawasumi and Beverly Yanez painting a paint-by-number image of parrots with the two delightful athletes, and we spoke about soccer in Seattle and their time in the women's league in Japan. We also talked about the best farmers markets in the city- which the nearby Lauren Barnes weighed in on. Finally- after two hours when our painting was done- one of the staff members at the hospital took a photo of the three of us, and I left.

Unfortunately for me, that was not where the story ended either. I was excited the entire time (because who would not be excited to paint-by-number with their favorite sports team?), but managed to maintain my composure throughout the event. After I left the hospital, I took a wrong turn somewhere without realizing it until five minutes later when I was standing in a parking lot I needed not enter. The place looked empty though, so I figured it was a good chance to dance and shout- and fist bump- the excitement out of my system. Then I turned around and found the Reign players standing behind me.

"Hi again," Beverly Yanez spoke to break the awkward silence.

"Hi!" I exclaimed in utter embarrassment. I then rushed past them through the door and promptly exited the hospital.

Podcasts also provide a great way for athletes to reach fans. The Seattle Reign's podcast "Coffee & Valkyries" began in 2018 as a way of discussing games and as a way for fans to get more information about the team's performances. The podcast turned into a mostly interview show where members of the team stopped by for the two hosts of the podcast to interview. Each interview involved questions about what the athletes like to do for fun in Seattle, what goals they had for the year, and about the quality of the team and the league. The NWSL ran a similar series of interviews with the "Lifetime Player Spotlight" where NWSL athletes gave short biographies about their lives.

On 11 August, the Reign had their next August match- this time against Utah under the smoke of nearby forest fires. The forest fires in Northern California, Colorado, and British Columbia were so destructive that smoke covered the Cascadia region- forcing the Reign-Royals game to include breaks for players to equip oxygen tanks to clear their lungs of ash. Seattle started the game with Megan Rapinoe, Jodie Taylor, Jasmyne Spencer, Morgan Andrews, Jess Fishlock, Allie Long, Christen Westphal, Lauren Barnes, Megan Oyster, Theresa Nielsen, and Lydia Williams.

During the first half, Seattle dominated possession with shots at the 11th, 13th, 17th, and 23rd minutes. Utah defense held however, and the first half ended in a scoreless tie. During the second half, Seattle continued to dominate possession, scoring early in the half at the 48th minute with a goal from Jess Fishlock off a Megan Oyster assist. The few Royals shots all met Lydia Williams saves, and the game ended in a 1-0 win for Seattle.

Around the league; Utah defeated Washington 1-0, North Carolina tied Chicago 1-1, Houston defeated New Jersey 2-1, and Portland defeated Orlando 2-0. Adriana Franch (Portland Thorns FC) earned both the Player of the Week and Save of the Week awards. Hayley Raso (Portland) earned the Goal of the Week award. If it seems like Portland wins a lot of these awards, that observation would not be incorrect.

Each week, the NWSL gives four options for both the Goal of the Week and Save of the Week awards for fans to vote on. Since Portland's team has the largest fan base in the world; anytime a Thorns player is eligible for one of the awards, they almost always win. Those two awards provide more information about the size of a team's fans than the quality of a goal or save. Out of the twenty-two weekly awards, Portland players won eight Goals of the Week and five Saves of the Week. The team with the second largest fan base- Orlando Pride- won six Goals of the Week and eight Saves of the Week.

In contrast, the North Carolina Courage won only one of each of the awards, but won the championship title. The Player of the Week award comes from the league itself and eliminates the unbalanced democracy of the league's fans. The Courage won six Players of the Week awards while Portland won three. Over the course of the season, Seattle won two Players of the Week awards, zero Goals of the Week, and zero Saves of the Week.

On 15 August, the Seattle Reign played a mid-week game against the Chicago Red Stars- another team eager to win games to advance their pursuit of the postseason. The Reign started the game with Jodie Taylor, Jasmyne Spencer, Jess Fishlock, Nahomi Kawasumi, Morgan Andrews, Allie Long, Christen Westphal, Lauren Barnes, Megan Oyster, Theresa Nielsen, and Lydia Williams.

Chicago dominated possession in the first half, but the Seattle defense held strong. Williams made important saves at the 8th, 9th, 18th, and 27th minutes to keep the game a scoreless tie going into the half. In the second half, Williams continued to make saves before Seattle finally thrust themselves into the offense in the last ten minutes of the game. The game ended in a scoreless draw- preventing either team from walking away victorious.

In other week twenty-one games, Houston defeated Washington 4-0, Utah tied New Jersey 2-2, Chicago tied Portland 2-2, and North Carolina defeated Orlando 3-0. Katie Johnson (Sky Blue FC) earned the Player of the Week award, Christine Sinclair (Portland Thorns FC) earned the Goal of the Week, and Ashlyn Harris (Orlando Pride) earned the Save of the Week.

Communication between a team and their fans is not always as simple as podcasts and Instagram photos. Teams and their athletes have to display only their best selves to their fans in order to grow. Those teams entirely transparent with less than stellar performances are more likely to lose fans. A 2009 study found women were more likely than men to feel inadequate at work and home- but have the double standard of losing social media fans if they admit it online. This inability to express accurate emotion can lead to anxiety and depression.[127] Some athletes in the NWSL however are trying to change that.

On World Suicide Prevention Day, Orlando Pride goalkeeper Ashlyn Harris opened up about a story of her own feelings of inadequacy. One day, Harris was boarding a team bus to leave a hotel for a Pride game when a fan approached Harris for an autograph. Harris politely explained to the fan that the athletes don't give out autographs outside of designated events, and- in response- the fan began spouting insults against the goalkeeper. For the entire game later that day, Harris could not shake feelings of anxiety as a direct result of the encounter. Harris told her story because she wanted others with similar stories to understand that it is alright to be open about difficult emotions; and that she hoped by telling her story, others might have the courage to tell theirs.[128]

On 21 August, the Reign would have their next August match against the Houston Dash. Seattle began the game with control of the ball- taking shots at the 3rd, 7th, and 9th minutes. Houston defense held out though, and the first half ended in a scoreless draw. During the second half, Seattle continued to dominate possession with Jodie Taylor scoring at the 58th minute off a Theresa Nielsen assist followed quickly by another Jodie Taylor goal at the 61st minute. After the second Seattle goal, Houston took control of the ball, but could not muster a goal. The game ended in a 2-0 win for the Reign.

Seattle then had a second week twenty-two game against the league-leading North Carolina Courage. Seattle started the game with Jasmyne Spencer, Jodie Taylor, Elizabeth Addo, Morgan Andrews, Jess Fishlock, Kristen McNabb, Steph Catley, Lauren Barnes, Megan Oyster, Theresa Nielsen, and Lydia Williams. North Carolina dominated possession in the first half- forcing Lydia Williams to make several saves for Seattle.

The Reign held on though and ended the half in a scoreless draw. In the second half, North Carolina continued their dominant offence. During a rare Seattle counter-attack, Theresa Nielsen scored for the Reign at the 67th minute to give Seattle the lead. In the last moments of stoppage time however, Lynn Williams scored a goal for North Carolina; and the game ended in a 1-1 tie.

---

[127] Marsh. 2016.
[128] Harris. 2018.

Week twenty-two saw several games with every team eager to win their final matches of the regular season. Utah defeated Washington 1-0, Portland defeated New Jersey 2-1, Chicago defeated Orlando 3-1, Portland defeated Washington 1-0, and Houston defeated New Jersey 6-1. Sam Kerr (Chicago Red Stars) earned the Player of the Week award while Tobin Heath (Portland Thorns FC) won the Goal of the Week and Ashlyn Harris (Orlando Pride) won the Save of the Week.

On 31 August, the national team players for the United States and Chile met for a friendly match. NWSL goals came from Christen Press (Utah Royals) at the 59th minute. A goal from a non-NWSL USA player and an own goal from a Chilean defender allowed the US to win 3-0. Elsewhere in the world, England qualified for the 2019 World Cup with NWSL players Jodie Taylor (Seattle Reign FC) and Rachel Daly (Houston Dash), and Canada defeated Brazil 1-0 with the help of NWSL player Nichelle Prince (Houston) scoring the game's sole goal.

Sam Kerr (Chicago Red Stars) would go on to receive the Player of the Month honors for August. The team of the month for August included goalkeeper Lydia Williams (Seattle Reign FC); defenders Abby Erceg (North Carolina Courage), Megan Oyster (Seattle), Theresa Nielsen (Seattle), and Taylor Comeau (Chicago); midfielders Vanessa DiBernardo (Chicago), Lindsey Horan (Portland Thorns FC), and Sophia Huerta (Houston Dash); and forwards Tobin Heath (Portland) and Lynn Williams (North Carolina).[129]

---

[129] Balf. 2018.

Chapter 4: Reign Without Weeping

"Call Your Girlfriend" Robyn

September began with continued international games bringing the triarii of the league out of play. The US defeated Chile once again with NWSL goals from Mallory Pugh (Washington Spirit), Tobin Heath (Portland Thorns FC), and Carli Lloyd (Sky Blue FC). Scotland qualified for their first Women's World Cup with help from NWSL player Rachel Corsie (Utah Royals). Rachel Daly (Houston Dash) scored a goal for England in a match against Kazakhstan before the national teams returned their NWSL players to the US league.

On 7 September, Seattle and Portland met again for another Cascadia Clash. Seattle started the game with Jasmyne Spencer, Jodie Taylor, Elizabeth Addo, Morgan Andrews, Jess Fishlock, Rumi Utsugi, Steph Catley, Lauren Barnes, Megan Oyster, Christen Westphal, and Lydia Williams. Portland dominated the first have without any counter-attacks from Seattle- although Jess Fishlock did score an early goal for the Reign in the 4th minute.

Williams worked hard to protect the goal with important saves at the 13th and 21st minutes, but a Portland goal at the 30th minute from Lindsey Horan tied the game. Another goal at the 45th minute nearly gave Portland the lead had the referees not voided the point as an off-side call. (Portland's coach appeared on television on the sidelines infuriated and hollering at referees with swear words fit only for sailors on the high seas.)

During the second half, Portland continued their attack with an early goal from Tobin Heath at the 49th minute, but Seattle finally counter-attacked. All of the shots fell off target however and gave Portland's forwards the opportunities they needed to resume their offensive. Lindsey Horan scored a goal off a corner kick at the 82nd minute, and the game ended in a 1-3 loss for the Reign.

Elsewhere in the league for the final regular season games, the Washington Spirit and Sky Blue FC tied 1-1, the Chicago Red Stars defeated New Jersey 5-0, New Jersey defeated the Orlando Pride 1-0 (their only win for the season), the Utah Royals defeated Chicago 2-1, and the North Carolina Courage defeated the Houston Dash 5-0. Lindsey Horan received the last Player of the Week award as well as the last Goal of the Week award while Nicole Barnhart earned the final Save of the Week award. Because September had only one week of regular season games, the month would have no Player of the Month or Team of the Month honors.

In the NWSL, several factors lead to a team's ability to advance to the postseason. From one end of the spectrum, having proper funding and facilities gives a team the ability to train healthier and engage a larger audience- which in turn helps inspire the athletes to perform at their best during every home game. Having referees well trained to give proper calls and prevent miscommunication on the field over penalties and fouls helps keep teams from receiving unfair calls that could sway victory on the field. Even the very genesis of a new team allows the owners and coaches to assemble the most effective group of players and train them in the pre-season to mold them into the style of play the team believes it needs to win.

Equally so, individual athletes make a team. The soul a player brings to the team and to the game- their dedication to practicing drills at home, their drive to keep playing through exhaustion, their choices to ignore pain and bloody noses in the desire to play the full ninety minutes- paired with each other player on the team ultimately rounds out the fate of a soccer team. There is a balance though between the team and the individual- such as a team that wants to focus on defensive plays and an athlete skilled in offensive action. This balance between societal desired behavior and self-identified pursuits is not unique to soccer either, and it is rarely balanced.

I will refer to the "balance" between societal and self-identification as "belonging" because within the context of the NWSL, an athlete only "belongs" to a team when there is a mutual agreement between athlete and team over the athlete's role on the roster and how the team will use the athlete during the season. Anthropologist Nira Yuval-Davis explained this definition of "belonging" as a combination of social locations, emotional attachments, and ethical and political values on the part of the individual; as well as participatory politics of citizenship and entitlement and status on the part of the group (or team in the case of the NWSL).[130]

When it comes to making the postseason, an NWSL team needs a strong sense of belonging (or partnership between individual and tribe mentalities) to coordinate their efforts and perform well enough to enter the final stage of competition. The 2013 season for the Seattle Reign was an example of how this sense of belonging could be unbalanced.

Only four Reign players from the 2013 season were still on the 2018 roster- Kiersten "The Ghost" Dallstream, Megan Rapinoe, Lauren Barnes, and Jess Fishlock (although Michelle Betos returned to the team in the 2018 season). The reason for their continued placement on the team came out of a mutual agreement of their role on the team. Every other member of the 2013 team either moved to another team (and in some cases other leagues), retired, or the team simply waived the players. Each of the four players have become staples of the team in their time in Seattle, and their self-identification altered during their time to find loyalty in the team that kept them for so long.

In the case of Jess Fishlock, the athlete spoke openly about how her time in both the NWSL and the Seattle Reign altered her sense of self-identification. The league's intense level of skill forced the athlete to constantly work hard on maintaining her athleticism- altering her personality to become an athlete that is always thinking about- and training for- every single game. On top of that, Fishlock has found identity in Seattle- especially with the family that hosted her. Fishlock gained a second family in Seattle through her host family who encouraged her to "be the best version [she] could be."[131]

"Bad At Love" Halsey

Based on their performances in the regular season, the North Carolina Courage, Portland Thorns FC, Seattle Reign FC, and the Chicago Red Stars entered the postseason. For each season of the NWSL, the top four teams at the end of the regular season enter the playoffs with the first and fourth teams playing against each other, and the second and third teams playing against each other in single-game semifinal matches. The top seed in each game would host the

---

[130] Yuval-Davis. 2006.
[131] Lifetime. 2018.

semifinal game- meaning North Carolina would host Chicago and Portland would host Seattle.

A late season hurricane forced a change of venue for the Courage-Red Stars game however, and- instead of having the teams play in a nearby stadium (Orlando or Washington) or in the other team's venue (Chicago)- somehow the Portland team managed to earn the right to host the two teams at their stadium. This meant Portland ended up hosting all three games of the postseason.

This also meant anyone with tickets to the game would have to either forfeit their money and not be within driving distance of the game, or dish out expensive last-minute plane tickets to Portland. On top of that inconvenience, the stadium's construction in Portland was not ready yet, so only half of the seats were available- and that was the half of the seating the cameras showed during the telecast of the game. That made it appear as though nobody was at the match to those watching online or on television.

The whole concept of a postseason in sports is an excellent example of societal constructions of identity. At the team level, a soccer team can play the best season of their existence in the NWSL and still not make the playoffs. This is largely because of what every other team is doing. I recall my own experience in sports growing up. While in high school I was attempting to qualify for the Junior Olympics for the sport of fencing.

Within fencing there are three separate sub-categories of competition (comparable to say track running where there is a 100 meter race, an 800 meter race, and several long-distance events). I attempted to qualify for two of the events and was substantially better at one than the other, but I failed to qualify in the event I was better at simply because there were other people who were better at the event than I was. I *did* however qualify for my worst event because there were less people trying to qualify, and those who were trying spent less time training for the event than I had.

This extends to soccer as well, and US Soccer- the main national organization for professional soccer in the United States- has taken notice. In 2018, US Soccer unveiled a new term with an experimental approach to athletic determinism based on societal and biological constructions of identity known as "Bio-Banding." What the organization's observations found was that within youth sports, children mature at different ages with some boys and girls going through puberty far before (or far after) the national average- giving unfair advantages or disadvantages in youth sports.

This inequality in physical maturity leads to post-pubescent youth gaining more endurance and strength while pre-pubescent youth are forced to make up for their weaknesses with increasing their skill training. This can lead towards bias among coaches in school sports dropping prepubescent athletes who may have the skills for the sport, but not the endurance of their post-pubescent pupils.[132]

This same alternation in development exists at the club-level as well. Even teams that have less of their 2013 players than the Reign (Portland Thorns had two 2013 players: Tobin Heath and Christine Sinclair), teams rarely alter their team as dramatically as the Seattle Reign have in their two "great extinctions" The Seattle Reign started the 2018 season with thirteen new players and a new head coach- a team far from experienced in terms of individuals working as a cohesive tribe.

Alternatively, the Seattle Reign's principles of staple non-allocated player veterans like Beverly Yanez and Lauren Barnes helped initiate a tribal nationalism among the team that united the new players, adopted the new coach, and set individual goals in tandem with the tribal pursuits for the team. Most sports statisticians would commend the Reign for advancing as far as they had as a relatively new team, but the secret to the team is their ability to dramatically shift personalities by regenerating into a new tribe historically in a single season.

After the first great extinction after the 2013 season, the Reign had two of their best seasons so far in the league- advancing to the finals in both 2014 and 2015. It would be Seattle's long-time rivals in Portland however that would be the Reign's ultimate weakness for the 2018 season. In 2018, the Cascadia Clash extended into the postseason for the first time in the six years of the NWSL, and Seattle would need to combat Portland in the Thorns' home turf.

Seattle started the game with Megan Rapinoe, Jodie Taylor, Jasmyne Spencer, Rumi Utsugi, Jess Fishlock, Allie Long, Steph Catley, Lauren Barnes, Megan Oyster, Theresa Nielsen, and Lydia Williams. Portland and Seattle harshly fought over the ball in the

---

[132] US Soccer. 2018.

first half with strong offensive plays from both teams. Lydia Williams made important saves at the 8th and 18th minutes before Jasmyne Spencer scored for Seattle at the 28th minute.

Tobin Heath scored an equalizer before the end of the half to make the game a 1-1 draw. In the second half, yellow cards rained down from referees with a card for Portland at the 50th minute and cards for Seattle at the 55th and 60th minutes. Lindsey Horan scored a goal at the 77th minute to give Portland the lead, and the game ended in a 1-2 loss for the Reign. Seattle's season was over, and the team returned to the Emerald City in defeat. Even with the societal label of defeat however, the individualism of self-identification disallowed Reign players to return home unhappy.

Perhaps the best example of the formidable strength of individual Reign player psyches comes from goalkeeper Lydia Williams. Williams grew up in Western Australia in a rural community to an American mother and an Aboriginal Australian father. The young Williams grew up with a dual identity and strongly identified with her indigenous roots, but she also grew up incredibly shy.

Soccer- and especially her role as a young goalkeeper- gave Lydia an opportunity to open up through learning the life skills of mental and physical strength as well as independence. Williams' father died when she was fifteen, and his last words to the young Lydia were that of pride and admiration. Williams said that one of the most important lessons her father taught her was that the most important thing in life was the love an individual has for their friends and family.[133]

When the team returned to Seattle, Reign players took to social media to express their support for their teammates and their admiration for how far they had advanced under their team's youthful condition. Even the team's 2014 roster hardly reflected the 2018 team. Apart from the four 2013 players, only two athletes from the 2014 team still served the Reign in their 2018 season: Beverly Yanez and Nahomi Kawasumi. A few days after the Thorns defeated the Reign, North Carolina defeated Chicago; and the two finalists for the championship game began to prepare for the final match of the 2018 season.

---

[133] Lifetime. 2018.

"October" Alessia Cara

In the finals, North Carolina went on to defeat Portland in the championship game and earned the season's championship trophy. Two sets of awards arrived shortly after the end of the season to award the best players in the league's sixth season. The top eleven players according to a league-wide social media vote were Adriana Franch (Portland Thorns FC), Rebecca Sonnett (Portland), Becky Sauerbrunn (Utah Royals FC), Abby Erceg (North Carolina Courage), Abby Dahlkemper (North Carolina), Tobin Heath (Portland), Lindsey Horan (Portland), McCall Zerboni (North Carolina), Crystal Dunn (North Carolina), Sam Kerr (Chicago Red Stars), and Megan Rapinoe (Seattle Reign FC).

The second best eleven were Lydia Williams (Seattle), Julie Ertz (Chicago), Emily Menges (Portland), Steph Catley (Seattle), Debhina (North Carolina), Carli Lloyd (Sky Blue FC), Christine Sinclair (Portland), Lynn Williams (North Carolina), Rachel Daly (Houston Dash), and Sophia Huerta (Houston).[134] Two Most Valuable Players were crowned after the game with the Championship MVP award going to Jessica McDonald (North Carolina) and the NWSL MVP award going to Lindsey Horan (Portland). Imani Dorsey (Sky Blue FC) earned the Rookie of the Year award, Paul Riley (North Carolina) earned the Coach of the Year award, Abby Erceg (North Carolina) earned the Defender of the Year, and Adrianna Franch (Portland) earned the Goalkeeper of the Year.

After the end of an NWSL season, each team immediately sets out to begin preparing for the next season- including adjusting their rosters. The earliest adjustments usually come during the regular season in the form of "waiving" players. Essentially, waiving an athlete is comparable to excommunication. The player is not traded to another team or loaned to another league. They do not retire, nor are they placed on a temporary absence (such as for a season-ending injury). The athlete is simply removed from the roster to make room for future draft picks or free agents. Hastati are typically those waived as well as rorarii.

---

[134] NWSL. 2018.

Seattle Reign athletes waived from the 2013 season included Kristina Larsen, Kristen Meier, and Emily van Egmond as well as Jenny Ruiz and Emily Zurrer- triarii who lost their "allocated player" status in the reconfiguring of league rules ahead of the 2014 season. In the following year; the Seattle Reign waived Megan Brigman, Holly Hein, and rorarii Abigail Steele (injury replacement player for Hope Solo), as well as triarii Stephanie Cox and Carmelina Moscato- who both lost their "allocated player status" from the US and Canadian National teams (respectively).

Ahead of the 2016 season, the Reign waived Katrine Veje, Caroline Stanley (whom New Jersey later signed), Antonia Goransson, and Paige Nielsen. In 2017, the Reign waived Michelle Cruz, rorarii Andi Tostanoski, and Michaela Hahn. Ahead of the 2018 season, the Reign waived Rachel Corsie (who later signed with the Utah Royals) and Larissa Crummer; waived Maddie Bauer mid-season; and waived triarii Adelaide Gay whose "allocated player" status ended with the US team.

What happens after a team waives a player is often left to the athlete to decide. In most occasions, the athlete attempts to find a team in the league to join. The majority of athletes end up needing to leave the US entirely to continue to play at the professional level. Emily van Egmond returned to Australia after leaving the Reign in 2013 and played in two seasons of the women's league there before moving to Germany to play in their league for the 2015 season. Van Egmond later joined the Australian National team for their second international season in 2016 at the Rio Olympics and scored two goals at the tournament.[135]

Carmelina Moscato left the Reign after the 2014 season and went to Australia to play in the women's league there. During the 2015/16 season, Moscato played for the Western Sydney Wanderers and scored her first goal in the league in a record-setting stoppage time game win.[136] Moscato would later rejoin the Canadian national team and was on their roster ahead of the 2019 Women's World Cup.

After the 2015 season, the Seattle Reign drafted then waived Paige Nielsen midway through the 2016 season. Nielsen left the

---

[135] Eckford. 2016.
[136] Moscato. 2015.

United States and played the remainder of the summer with Apollon Ladies in Cyprus before joining the Western Sydney Wanderers in Australia later in the year.[137] Nielsen would later leave Australia to play in the women's league in South Korea.

Rorarii Andi Tostanoski left the Seattle Reign after the NWSL began a new policy of only allowing "amateur" athletes during World Cup qualifying years- ending the policy of having back-up players on teams, and only allowing a small number of National Team Replacement Players and for single-season contracts. As a result, Tostanoski lost her place in the league. In response, the young goalkeeper took up a new role as a Graduate Assistant Goalkeeper Coach at Hawaii Pacific University for the women's soccer team.[138]

Ahead of the 2018 season, the Reign waived Rachel Corsie whom the new Utah Royals FC team later picked up. Corsie was by no means a hastati of the Reign. The defender was a staple of the team since 2015- making her a rare waived principe in the Reign's history. Part of why the Royals picked up Corsie was because of the long-time former Reign coach Laura Harvey had returned from retirement for the opportunity to coach the new Salt Lake City team and needed recognizable faces on her roster.[139] Corsie would go on to serve as a formidable force as a defender for Utah during the 2018 season.

"Home With You" Madison Beer

After the end of the NWSL season, triarii in the league began preparing for the final matches that would determine whether they would enter the 2019 Women's World Cup. For countries in North America and the Caribbean, this would culminate in the October CONCACAF Women's Championship tournament. The tournament would pit the nations of the United States, Mexico, Trinidad & Tobago, Panama, Canada, Jamaica, Costa Rica, and Cuba against each other for entrance into the 2019 Women's World Cup.

The international level of play forces players from even the most bitter of club-level rivalries to work together as teammates-

---

[137] Western Sydney Wanderers FC. 2016.
[138] Hawaii Pacific University. 2018.
[139] Utah Royals FC. 2018.

meaning Reign players Megan Rapinoe and Allie Long would soon play beside Tobin Heath and Lindsey Horan. This is part of what gives the triarii class of players the strength to lead and guide the teams on the field in the club level.

There, Rapinoe and Long have the power to keep the hastati on the team reserved under the pressure of the game. When club-level teammates face off against each other on opposing international teams (such as Adriana Leon of Canada and Jodie Taylor of England), those same triarii help maintain friendly play at the international level. The balance of international and club-level play helps maintain peace among both international and club-level leagues.

In mid-September US Soccer announced their roster for the tournament, which included several NWSL players. This included Ashlyn Harris (Orlando Pride), Alyssa Naeher (Chicago Red Stars), Abby Dahlkemper (North Carolina Courage), Crystal Dunn (North Carolina), Kelley O'Hara (Utah Royals FC), Becky Sauerbrunn (Utah), Casey Short (Chicago), Rebecca Sonnett (Portland Thorns FC), Morgan Brian (Chicago), Julie Ertz (Chicago), Lindsey Horan (Portland), Rose Lavelle (Washington Spirit), and Kristie Mewis (North Carolina).[140]

Canada announced their roster would include Lindsey Agnew (Houston Dash), Allysha Chapman (Houston), Shelina Zadorski (Orlando), Rebecca Quinn (Washington), Diana Matheson (Utah), Adriana Leon (Seattle), Nichelle Prince (Houston), and Christine Sinclair (Canada).[141] Mexico announced their roster would include Bianca Henninger (Houston), Christina Murillo (Chicago), and Katie Johnson (New Jersey).[142]

The non-allocated players in the NWSL prepared for something else. Teams can begin trading players as soon as their season ends. In 2013, The Reign began making trades ahead of their second season on 10 September when they traded Kaylyn Kyle away to the Boston Breakers in exchange for Carmela Moscato. Further trades ahead of the 2014 season included trading away Renee

---

[140] Purdy. 2018.
[141] Purdy. 2018.
[142] Purdy. 2018.

Cuellar, Kristie Mewis, Michelle Betos, Christine Nairn, Jessica McDonald, Liz Bogus, Nikki Marshall, and Niki Cross.

Ahead of the 2015 season, the Reign traded away Kate Deines, Amanda Frisbie, and Sydney Leroux. Ahead of the 2016 season, the Reign traded away Amber Brooks, and Meghan Klingenberg (after receiving her in a trade). Ahead of the 2017 season, the Reign traded away Havana Solaun. Ahead of the 2018 season, the Reign traded away Rebekah Stott, Katie Johnson, Diana Matheson, Carson Pickett, Christine Nairn, Haley Kopmeyer, and Merritt Mathias.

Luckily with trades, what happens to an athlete after leaving a team is fairly easy to track. Additionally, there is a possibility for an athlete to return to the Reign. This happened with Michelle Betos and Christine Nairn who both came back to Seattle to play at least one more season with the team. On the other end of the spectrum, an athlete could bounce around several teams without any hopes of settling in one city for more than one season.

For Jessica McDonald- whom the Seattle Reign traded away following the 2013 season- the athlete considered quitting professional soccer at the end of every season with the NWSL before settling in North Carolina. Between 2013 and 2016, McDonald played on five separate NWSL teams. In 2016 however, McDonald earned a spot on the USWNT. She only played in one game though and another in 2017 before joining the North Carolina Courage. In 2018, McDonald earned the Championship MVP award.[143]

Amanda Frisbie was another player that drifted from team to team following her departure from the Reign. The Seattle Reign drafted her in 2014, but traded her after a season-ending injury forced her to miss the season. She first played in a match for the Western New York Flash in 2015 before moving to FC Kansas City. In the 2016 season, Frisbie had to leave the US after Kansas City waived her, so she went to Iceland's women's league before returning to the NWSL to play for the Boston Breakers. After one season with the Breakers, Boston's team folded and Sky Blue FC picked her up during the dispersal draft.[144]

---

[143] Tannenwald. 2018.
[144] Sky Blue FC. 2018.

After Amber Brooks' 2015 season, the Reign traded the athlete to the Houston Dash and stayed with the team through the league's sixth season. In her first season with the team, Brooks scored one goal and two assists. During the 2017 season, Brooks was one of four players in the league to play 2160 minutes in the regular season. Brooks was also one of only a few 2018 NWSL players who has played in all six seasons of the league.[145]

After the 2016 season, the Seattle Reign traded Havana Solaun to the Washington Spirit. In the 2017 season, Solaun was the only Spirit player to appear in every one of her team's regular season games. While with the Reign, Solaun played in only six matches (as opposed to twenty-four), but scored a game-winning goal in a 12 June match against the Houston Dash.[146]

After two seasons with the Reign, the Seattle team traded Carson Pickett to the Orlando Pride ahead of the 2018 season. The donut loving soccer player settled in well in Orlando. Pickett uses her "unique" status as a disabled athlete to push herself to rise to a higher standard than many of her peers. The one-armed player refuses to say "no" or "can't" which gave her the confidence to accept her new team and found a way to carve a spot for herself on the field. Pickett's move to Orlando also had the side effect of the athlete partnering with an organization that creates prosthetic limbs for disabled children.[147]

"2002" Anne-Marie

In the first round of the CONCACAF Championship tournament, the United States defeated Mexico 6-0 on 4 October with NWSL goals from Megan Rapinoe (Seattle Reign), Julie Ertz (Chicago Red Stars), Alex Morgan (Orlando Pride), and Tobin Heath (Portland Thorns). Panama defeated Trinidad & Tobago 3-0. Canada would later defeat Jamaica 2-0 with NWSL goals from Nichelle Prince (Houston Dash). Costa Rica would also defeat Cuba 8-0.[148]

---

[145] Houston Dash. 2018.
[146] Washington Spirit. 2018.
[147] Lifetime. 2018.
[148] Purdy. 2018.

Across the Atlantic, European NWSL triarii began squaring off in the UEFA play-offs with the Netherlands defeating Denmark 2-0 (including Seattle's Theresa Nielsen for Denmark) and Belgium and Switzerland tying 2-2 (including Portland's Ana-Maria Crnogorcevic for Switzerland). An additional international game featuring NWSL players would include France defeating Australia 2-0 (including Portland's Ellie Carpenter and Cailtin Foord, Seattle's Steph Catley and Elise Kellond-Knight, and Houston's Clare Polkinghorne and Kyah Simon for Australia).[149]

Some athletes leave the NWSL during the offseason to play in leagues in other countries. This is referred to as a "loan." While a player is on load to another league, their NWSL team may trade the rights to the athlete to another team. Typically, only non-allocated players are loaned to other leagues since national team athletes typically need to prepare for international games and limit their risk of major injuries. Over the six seasons of the NWSL, the league slowly wove itself with the women's league in Australia (since the two leagues have opposite seasons)- sending several athletes from each NWSL team to the Australian league.

Records for off-season loans begins with the 2015 season (2015/16 season for the Australian league). Six athletes left the NWSL in 2015 to play in the Australian league on-loan: Rachel Corsie, Jess Fishlock, Kendall Fletcher, Haley Kopmeyer, Kim Little, and Keelin Winters. Five 2016 Reign players left the team to play in other leagues on-loan with Lauren Barnes, Jess Fishlock, Kendall Fletcher, and Beverly Yanez playing in Australia; and Nahomi Kawasumi playing in Japan. In 2017, eight Reign players left Seattle to play on-loan in other leagues with Lauren Barnes, Larissa Crummer, Jess Fishlock, Haley Kopmeyer, Kristen McNabb, Carson Pickett, Rebekah Stott, and Lydia Williams all playing in Australia.

The W-League in Australia reached its tenth season when the NWSL finished its sixth. In those ten years, there have been major milestones in the sport; which may be what attracts NWSL athletes to the league. 2018 Seattle Reign player Steph Catley is listed as the 8th in most appearances in W-League games and fourth in most winning appearances. 2018 Chicago Red Stars player Sam Kerr is

---

[149] Purdy. 2018.

listed as 2nd in most goals and tied for second in most goals in a single season. Seattle Reign player Jodie Taylor also made the latter list. 2018 Seattle Reign's Lydia Williams tops the list for most clean sheets for a goalkeeper with Michelle Betos in 9th place and Orlando Pride's Haley Kopmeyer in 11th place.[150]

There are nine teams in the W-League; Adelaide United FC, Brisbane Roar FC, Canberra United, Melbourne City FC, Melbourne Victory, Newcastle United, Perth Glory, Sydney FC, and Western Sydney Wanderers. The league partners with several international online broadcasters including Oz.com for Oceania, East and Southeast Asia, Central and Eastern Europe, and East Africa; Kwese Sports which broadcasts across West and Central Africa; BT Sport in the UK; Pasifika TV in Oceania; and Sky Sport in New Zealand.

The future of the NWSL may mirror the present of the Australian League. Eight to nine teams seems to be the standard for single-country women's leagues, and a system of loaning players exists in several other sports for both men and women. Several NBA and WNBA players play in either Russia or China during the offseason. Playing in other leagues during the offseason also allows a player to experiment with their game having one league work as a practice season to prepare them for the coming NWSL regular season.

Continuing in the CONCACAF Championship, on 7 October the United States defeated Panama 5-0 with NWSL goals from Sam Mewis (North Carolina Courage), Carli Lloyd (Sky Blue FC), and Christen Press (Utah Royals). Mexico defeated Trinidad and Tobago 4-1 with one NWSL goal from Katie Johnson (New Jersey).[151] The next day, Jamaica defeated Costa Rica 1-0 and Canada defeated Cuba 12-0 with NWSL goals from Adriana Leon (Seattle Reign FC), Rebecca Quinn (Washington Spirit), Christine Sinclair (Portland Thorns FC), and Diana Matheson (Utah).[152]

In Europe, Ana Crnogorcevic (Portland Thorns FC) led Switzerland with two wins against Belgium to advance to the UEFA finals. Theresa Nielsen (Seattle Reign FC) and Denmark fell to the Netherlands after two losses.[153] Elsewhere, Clare Polkinghorne

---

[150] Westfield W-League. 2018.
[151] Balf. 2018.
[152] Purdy. 2018.

(Houston Dash) scored for Australia in a friendly match against England that ended in a 1-1 draw.[154]

"Not Above Love" AlunaGeorge

World Cup and Olympic qualifying tournaments act as rituals during which those athletes in the principe class have the opportunity to "level up" and become triarii. Typically, the most renowned among the upper echelon are those triarii who are on national teams strong enough to enter either the World Cup or the Olympics with the highest tier of triarii being those of the Canadian and US national teams due to their special position within the league. When a long-time triarii of the league no longer finds themselves on a national team (such as retirement from international play or from their respective nation waving them from their national roster), that athlete begins the slow process towards retirement from professional soccer.

Retirement is essentially the opposite of waiving a player. A team waives a player to initiate their exit from a team while an athlete announces retirement to announce their exit from a team. Occasionally, some athletes that "retire" return to play on other teams or in other leagues. Sometimes a player who retires becomes an assistant coach for a team or head coach for a university. Others retire to focus on their role on their nation's national team while others simply leave the game and start new lives in graduate school or desired careers.

None of the Seattle Reign players from the 2013 or 2014 rosters retired following the respective seasons. Following the 2015 season, Mariah Bullock retired from the Reign and Danielle Foxhoven chose not to renew her contract with the Reign and left the NWSL. In August 2016, Hope Solo took an indefinite leave of absence (akin to retirement from soccer). At the end of the 2016 season, Keelin Winters, Manon Melis, and Lindsay Elston (later signing with the Boston Breakers) all retired with Kendall Fletcher leaving to pursue graduate school. At the end of the 2017 season, Elli Reed and Madylyn Schiffel both retired from the Reign.

---

[153] Purdy. 2018.
[154] Bakowski. 2018.

After choosing to not renew her contract with the Seattle Reign, Danielle Foxhoven remained in Seattle under a new role. The former soccer player became a soccer coach for a skills training organization known as Pro Skills Soccer. The service provides retired professional soccer players as coaches for hire to soccer programs throughout the Seattle area and partners closely with the Seattle Reign.[155]

Foxhoven is an interesting player for the history of the Reign for another reason. The athlete was about to start playing professional soccer for the first time in the US with the WPS (the second attempt at a women's league) before receiving a message from her agent that the league folded. Foxhoven scoured the world for a professional league to join to continue playing and eventually (and finally) found a team in the Russian' women's league that would accept her.

The team abused the athlete though- along with the other athletes of the team- by never paying the promised paycheck and giving the athletes performance enhancing drugs against their consent. The NWSL provided Foxhoven an avenue for returning to the US where the pay- regardless of how low it was- was at least dependable and where coaches and team owners did not force steroids on their players.[156]

After Keelin Winters retired in September of 2016, the Reign player continued to live in the Seattle area and eventually became a firefighter with the Kirkland Fire Department. Like with attempting to join the NWSL, there are thousands of applicants trying to become firefighters in the Seattle area annually. Winters had to compete for the chance to join the three-month long training course before taking a test to determine her fate. The process was nothing new for the veteran soccer player though and Keelin Winters was still fighting fires in the Seattle area during the 2018 NWSL season.[157]

After retiring from the Seattle Reign in September 2017, long-time Reign player Elli Reed accepted a job offer with the University of Portland as the Women's Soccer Director of Operations. Reed had played for the university while a student there

---

[155] Foxhoven. 2018.
[156] Ibid. Oxenham. 2017.
[157] Seattle Reign FC. 2018.

before joining the professionals in 2011 and was happy to receive the job offer from her old college. Reed continued her work with Water 1st International, Pro Skills Soccer, and Z Girls after accepting the new job.[158]

NWSL athletes on the US national team for the Rio Olympics not included on the roster ahead of the CONCACAF Championship included Hope Solo ([formerly] Seattle Reign FC), Whitney Engen ([formerly] Boston Breakers), and Allie Long (Seattle).[159] The CONCACAF roster only provided twenty spots while a world cup roster allows twenty-three, so Long will likely find a spot on the team for the world cup, but Whitney Engen and Hope Solo are excellent examples for how leaving a national team can lead to retirement from league play.

---

[158] University of Portland. 2018.
[159] US Soccer. 2016.

Chapter 5: Making the Reign Familiar and the Familiar Reign

"Unravel Me" Sabrina Claudio

The world of American Anthropology is changing. For a long time, even those anthropologists with the best intentions were engaging in colonialist behavior- like Franz Boas inviting himself into an Inuit Community or Margaret Mead inviting herself into Samoan culture. For the most part these studies served to fascinate Western audiences; but Boas provided little support for the evolving Inuit community, and Mead rarely revisited the Samoan girls she wrote about in *Coming of Age in Samoa*.

The world is rapidly changing around us as well, and the role of anthropology is changing to meet the demands of that change over such a short time. Anthropologists are traveling throughout the atolls of the Pacific Ocean to record folktales of cultures that will soon leave the sinking islands and assimilate into whatever nations they immigrate to where they will eventually forget their oral stories. Other anthropologists are at the forefront of the changing definitions of race, gender, and religion. Others march in the street beside political protestors and others engage in studies to determine the ethics of medical and psychological research.

Usually, an anthropologist would take this time in the final pages of their ethnography to make one final case for what their research meant or why it was important. Instead, I want to make these pages about the people that were important and what they meant to the team. Whether they played in every game or supported the team from the sidelines, every member of the 2018 Seattle Reign was critical to their performance in the season; so I want to give the readers one final list of the athletes who made up the 2018 Seattle Reign roster- arranged via my categorization of hastati (new, non-national team Reign players), principes (veteran, non-national team Reign players), triarii (athletes on national team rosters), and rorarii (national team replacement players).

Hastati included Yael Averbuch (from FC Kansas City); Jasmyne Spencer (from Orlando Pride); Megan Oyster, Morgan Andrews, and Christen Westphal (from Boston Breakers), and Alyssa Kleiner (from Washington Spirit). Athletes Seattle drafted who did not appear in the season (for various reasons) included Ally Haran (Wake Forest University- college draft), Celia Jimenez Delgado (University of Alabama- college draft), and Lindsay Elston [who would have returned to the Reign as a principe] (Boston Breakers- dispersal draft). Yael Averbuch appeared in one game, Spencer in twenty-three, Oyster in twenty-one, Andrews in sixteen, Westphal in twelve, and Kleiner in ten. Jasmyne Spencer scored two goals and Oyster scored one.

Principes included Lauren Barnes (sixth season with Seattle, Big Woman, and co-captain), Kiersten "The Ghost" Dallstream (sixth season with Seattle), Beverly Yanez (fifth season with Seattle and Big Woman), Michelle Betos (second season with Seattle), Kristen McNabb (second season with Seattle), and Maddie Bauer [whom the team waived mid-season] (second season with Seattle). Lauren Barnes appeared in twenty games, Dallstream in three, Yanez in twenty, Betos in eight, McNabb in twenty, and Bauer in one. Beverly Yanez scored two goals.

Triarii included Lydia Williams and Steph Catley(Australia), Allie Long and Megan Rapinoe (USA), Theresa Nielsen (Denmark), Nahomi Kawasumi and Rumi Utsugi (Japan), Jess Fishlock (Wales, co-captain), Elizabeth Addo (Ghana), Adriana Leon (Canada), and Jodie Taylor (England). Adelaide Gay acted as the rorarii for Lydia Williams [though only until the end of April] and Jaycie Johnson acted as the rorarii for all other national team players [until signing a contract as a standard player in mid-July].

Lydia Williams appeared in seventeen games, Long in twenty, Catley in seventeen, Nielsen in twenty-one, Kawasumi in fourteen, Fishlock in nineteen, Addo in thirteen, Leon in six, Taylor in twenty-five, Rapinoe in seventeen, and Utsugi in sixteen. Allie Long scored three goals, Nielsen scored one, Fishlock scored two, Taylor scored nine, Rapinoe scored seven, and Utsugi scored one. Jaycie Johnson appeared in three games.[160]

The average game appearances for Seattle Reign hastati added up to 13.8 games with hastati scoring three total goals in the season. The average principe appeared in 12 games with two total goals. (Big Women appeared in an average of twenty games and scored a total of two goals.) The average triarii appeared in 16.8

---

[160] NWSL. 2018.

games with twenty-three total goals, and the average rorarii appeared in 3 games without goals. [I counted both rorarii as a single figure due to their combined fractions of the season only equaling roughly one season.]

From outside of the perspective of the Seattle Reign as a soccer team and the NWSL as a sports league, the Reign are a tribe within the kingdom of the NWSL- a kingdom without a king and a steward of the throne overworked to the point of vassals and warlords of the tribes gaining unbalanced power. In cultures throughout history and across the world, these situations are what cause regimes to collapse.

The problem is that the National Women's Soccer League is the third attempt at a dependable women's soccer league in the United States, and all signs pointed to its dependability cracking. Perhaps one day, the NWSL will fold just like the previous leagues. If that were to happen, everyone that invested their lives in the league would once again have the identity crisis of what to do next.

Whether that athlete is from the Reign, the Red Stars, or even the Portland Thorns; not one athlete in the NWSL deserves to be told they can no longer play soccer. The situation is akin to someone finding out their country no longer exists and they can never return home- that "sorry, it just didn't work out this time" message. This book helps illustrate the humanity in a culture many people see only a small fragment of.

Within the spectrum of sports, viewers often only see what athletes do on the field or maybe on social media, but the finite details of the everyday lives of women in the NWSL helps illustrate the concepts of tribal nationalism that can exist within a larger society through the bitter Cascadia Clash rivalry. It details the complexity of human commerce through the trading of players.

Perhaps- more than anything else- the study's greatest benefit was not what it provided for the study of anthropology. Instead, its greatest benefit was what the league gave to me. The most important lesson in Margaret Mead's *Coming of Age in Samoa* was not what the study said about the young women of Samoa, but what Margaret Mead learned from them. In all the strange blue smoke following Reign goals, the scavenger hunt for the haunted soda machine in Seattle, the dancing, the orange soccer cleats, time on inflatable canoes, and eating stadium concessions- I found myself.

I never imagined my career would revolve around women's sports, but it all began with the Seattle Reign. For some, their lives have slowly changed for the better as a result of the NWSL's several teams. Athletes in universities across the country no longer need to grapple with a reality where they cannot play the sport they love after graduation. If they choose to do so, they can attempt to become professional soccer players. Fans can take their families to games and instill in their children, siblings, or- in my case cousin- a sense of pride in their city's soccer team.

When setting out to write this book, I constantly questioned some of the topics I wrote about in my field journal. I wondered if I should add a section about sexual assault, I pondered the ethics of detailing my complaints about inequality between teams, and even thought about carefully wording a massive amount of this book to make sure I did not get any angry emails from the league office. (I actually still think I might get some of those emails.) I remembered what my mom told me though- to make the book about the people- about the athletes.

The NWSL is doing its best. I will in no way criticize the league for what they do or how they do what they are doing. They face a difficult task of creating and maintaining a high-quality professional soccer league capable of providing viewers with the soccer they deserve to see. They do so with almost no money, slow leadership, and unbalanced power among the several teams. With increased decentralization of power in the league, teams with large fan bases and extra money will only continue to steal power from the less powerful teams and could ultimately be the cause of destruction for the league.

That makes it even more difficult for athletes on teams like the former Western New York Flash or the Boston Breakers to come forward with stories of abuse- knowing their stories will probably find no empathetic audience. In anthropology, while researchers are tasked with using the tool of cultural relativism (learning to see the behaviors of a culture through that culture's perspective), it is never the role of an anthropologist to excuse toxic behaviors.

"Beautiful People" Andreya Triana

As much ill as I speak about the Portland Thorns from the perspective of the other end of the Cascadia Clash, I do have to recognize the organization is the model for success all other teams need in order to keep the NWSL from folding. Essentially, the Thorns were able to convince the men's soccer team's fans to show up to their games, which filled the stadium and made Thorns games popular to attend- and peer pressure works. Fans in every sports league across the country tend to favor the most popular team if they do not have one in their own town or region. On top of that, the Thorns have not historically had the best players (something that is usually well rounded in the league), nor have they had the greatest coach. (Actually Mark Parsons is a great coach.

He may yell at referees, but he does deserve credit. Statistically though, Laura Harvey is probably the best regular season coach through win/loss records, and Vlatko Andonovski is statistically the best season-long coach with the most championship titles.) The Thorns simply have an insane quantity and quality of fans. The Riveteers mob Providence Park and create an impossibly high revenue for the team, which can then use the money to increase the quality of facilities and travel arrangements for players. That money also feed the league and give an imbalance in favor towards the team.

Unfortunately, not every team in the NWSL can have what Portland has. In Portland, there is a professional men's basketball team, a professional men's soccer team, and a professional women's soccer team. Those three are it. In Seattle, there is professional baseball, professional football, professional men's soccer, professional women's basketball, and professional women's soccer.

Five teams overwhelm fans. Especially in seasons where the other teams are doing well, fans would love to go to every team's games. That's just not financially feasible. In Chicago, the Red Stars are competing with the NBA, the WNBA, two baseball teams, a football team, and a men's hockey team. So if the NWSL plans on expanding, the best route to go in to find financially productive teams would be to find cities with limited sports.

St. Louis for example has only men's hockey and baseball. It's rivalry with Chicago in baseball could also help fuel a second NWSL rivalry between the cities that would help stock the stadiums of both teams. Unfortunately heat indexes play a role as well since the league plays in the hottest part of the year. Games in Houston and Orlando often have to occur late in the day to prevent heat exhaustion among players. More northern teams could fare well then, such as a team in Colorado (like Colorado Springs with a population twice as large as Rochester, New York where the Western New York Flash played).

Alternatively, perhaps US Soccer should simply enact a rule that every men's soccer team must partner with a women's soccer team in the NWSL. Major League Soccer teams exist in Colorado Rapids, Dallas, Houston, two in Los Angeles, Minneapolis, Portland, Salt Lake City, San Jose, Seattle, Kansas City, Vancouver, Atlanta, Chicago, Columbus, Washington DC, Montreal, Boston, two in New York City, Orlando, Philadelphia, and Toronto. Every NWSL team that partners with a men's team (Portland Thorns, Utah Royals, Houston Dash, and Orlando Pride) all have the highest attendance of teams in the NWSL. The rule would not be revolutionary either.

Soccer journalist Gwendolyn Oxenham reported on a new rule in South American Football Confederation that required all men's teams to have a partner women's team by 2019- becoming the first soccer league in the world to establish such a rule.[161] If US Soccer actually committed to ensuring equal play for women in the US, this would instantly fortify the NWSL for several more seasons as well as encourage more fans to attend games. (Although North Carolina and New Jersey do not have MLS teams, all other NWSL teams- Chicago, Washington DC, and Seattle- could easily partner with their men's teams.)

One strength the league has is that it has proven it has at least some amount of staying power- meaning it will continue for at least two more seasons. One of the largest issues with the league is the low pay for athletes makes trades financially difficult to the degree that some athletes retire from soccer altogether to avoid the cost of moving to a new team. Instead of signing single-season contracts with players, two-year minimum contracts would give an athlete time to save money for a possible move.

More important than any of these improvements however is one major solution necessary for keeping the league intact. There needs to be a league commissioner. (I had to fight the urge to not type that last sentence in all caps.) Without strong, central governing; the NWSL is rapidly decentralizing into several teams

---

[161] Ibid. Oxenham. 2017.

becoming unbalanced in power and authority of league-wide decisions with the most popular teams becoming the proverbial war chiefs ruling on their own authority.

A similar series of events played out in 17th Century Japan. At the time, an emperor ruled Japan- though largely from a reserved and withdrawn position of decentralized power. The majority of Japan's leadership fell on warlord-led families (or shogunates). In the 17th Century, one shogunate- the Tokugawa- slowly rose to power through a combination of annexation, warfare, and politics to become the dominant, unofficial power in the empire. While the Tokugawa successes allowed the empire to enjoy its longest period of peace and prosperity, the side effect was an imbalance of power and continued decentralization of power from the imperial court.[162]

Teams like the Washington Spirit, Chicago Red Stars, and even the Seattle Reign do not have partnering men's teams. It is not popular to be a Sky Blue FC fan. It's not popular to go to a Spirit game, and it is not popular to wear a Seattle Reign jersey. That's all the more reason to watch them. Without the massive funding like the Pride receive and without the massive fan base like the Thorns have; three unpopular teams made up seventy-five percent of the 2018 NWSL postseason.

Although to be fair to Portland again, Gwendolyn Oxenham reported on a particular game between the Chicago Red Stars and the Portland Thorns during which Chicago fans repeatedly shouted disrespectful insults at Thorns players throughout the game. Also according to Oxenham, Thorns fans also shout "Fuck you, Seattle" during Cascadia Clash games though.[163] (So I don't feel much empathy for the Riveteers.)

One major aspect of why the majority of NWSL teams get low audience is because- within the context of United States popular culture- watching sports is largely either a male or family activity. Single women hardly ever go to sports games. In a 2014 study, sports researchers surveyed 2241 sports viewers with roughly equal participation in the study between men and women. Thirty-seven percent of those surveyed reported they watch baseball with forty-seven percent being male and twenty-seven percent being female.[164]

---

[162] Asia for Educators. 2018.
[163] Ibid. Oxenham. 2017.

One major reason for the massive discrepancy may return to sexual harassment and assault. A 2018 study found that college sexual assaults increase dramatically on game days for men's football games with fifteen percent of reported cases happening on away game days and forty-one percent occurring on home game days.[165] With numbers that high, it makes no sense then for a women's soccer league to focus on reaching a demographic (viewers of men's sports) to define their own fan base unless they wish to create the same toxic culture within the NWSL that includes increased rates of sexual assault.

The other demographic of sports fans are families. In Australia, the women's league for Australian Rules Football focuses instead on the family demographic, and it worked. Stadiums in 2017 consistently sold out. The approach made the games safer for single female attendees and made parents feel more comfortable bringing their children to games. The crowds were more respectful to opposing teams and each other, more diverse, and used less offensive language than the equivalent men's league games.[166]

During my time watching the World Surf League, anytime men's and women's surfing events occurred at the same location (such as in San Clemente, California), the crowd was measurably more sexually aggressive towards both female athletes and female audience. When women's events were in separate locations from men's events (such as Honolua Bay, Hawaii) the audience was more respectful of athletes- and even more likely to speak with pride about their own sisters, daughters, and friends competing in women's sports. That's no surprise for surfing though. The World Surf League has been actively working to close the gender pay gap and decrease sexism in surf culture for years.

In 2018, the World Surf League announced it would pay male and female surfers equally for equal performances in international surfing beginning with the 2019 season. At the beginning of the 2018 season, men who won a Championship Tour event (like division one soccer) earned one hundred thousand dollars per win while women earned only sixty-five thousand for equivalent

---

[164] Statista. 2014.
[165] Harvey. 2018.
[166] Jarrett. 2017.

wins. In contrast, the French men's soccer team won thirty-eight million dollars for winning the FIFA Men's World Cup in 2018 while the US women's soccer team earned only two million for winning the FIFA Women's World Cup in 2015.[167]

Opposed to Portland Thorns and Chicago Red Stars patriarchal fans that spill over from men's sports are the Reign family fan base. From my own experience of speaking with them, seeing them at games, and sharing meals at halftime and drinks in the beer garden; the Reign fans may be less numerous than the Riveteers, but no one is ever made to feel unwelcome- even fans of other teams.

Because of the great extinctions of the team, Reign fans constantly cheer on athletes on opposing teams- and are probably even wearing their jerseys. Reign fans bring their families and work hard to make minority groups feel welcome like through their long partnership with Athlete Ally. When there is a rare toxic attendee shouting obscenities at referees, it's the fans who tell the person to be more respectful before stadium security ever reaches the person.

People who live in Seattle can identify with their soccer team. The Reign are tucked away in the center of the city in a disguised arena that can actually be hard to find for someone if they do not know where to look. The team is akin to a tech-geek's hidden past as a high school grunge garage band member- a Microsoft employee that people would be surprised to learn can shred a bass guitar.

People are often surprised to learn Seattle has a women's soccer team, but they are also surprised when they see the Reign play. Even with a team of mostly new players from several different clubs and a new head coach, the team ended the 2018 season in third place- and all with an average of about five thousand fans per game. Imagine what they could do with seventeen thousand fans per game.

I noticed a similarity between the story of the Seattle Reign and the F Scott Fitzgerald short story of *The Curious Case of Benjamin Button*. In Fitzgerald's story, the main character is born as an old man and becomes younger as time goes on. A 2008 film expanded on the story with actor Brad Pitt portraying the titular character. The story establishes a metaphor for a youth with the

---

[167] Wamsley. 2018.

mindset of an elder who- as he ages- slowly learns to find value in youthful life practices and focus on attracting children and teens to games (who will ultimately drag their parents with them).

The film adaptation of the story begins with a scene of a blind clockmaker in New Orleans tasked with making the main clock for a new train station. The clockmaker- whose son died in battle during World War I- made a clock whose hands moved counter-clockwise with the clockmaker explaining he hoped it may someday allow his battle-dead son to return to him one day. The film's ending scene depicts Benjamin Button's daughter reading a series of notes the main character wrote to her throughout her life that she was reading finally for the first time as an adult at her mother's deathbed.

The final note Button wrote to his daughter read, "For what it's worth: it's never too late or, in my case, too early to be whoever you want to be. There's no time limit, stop whenever you want. You can change or stay the same, there are no rules to this thing. We can make the best or the worst of it. I hope you make the best of it. And I hope you see things that startle you. I hope you feel things you never felt before. I hope you meet people with a different point of view. I hope you live a life you're proud of. If you find that you're not, I hope you have the courage to start all over again."[168]

The NWSL seems like a league aging in reverse. It started with everything it needed to survive past a third season- largely because it understood the failures of past league and could begin its first season with borrowed experience. As the seasons went on, the veteran athletes that started the league as players who had played in previous leagues slowly retired from the NWSL; and the league became younger and younger- and that may be what the clubs need.

Portland certainly does not need to prove their worth anymore, and Chicago is the location of the league's headquarters. Orlando and Salt Lake City have learned to love their teams. As long as the league can support players on teams that fold or move by paying for the cost of travel for athletes on moving teams and continuing to add new teams to the league roster, the NWSL will continue on.

The Seattle Reign started in 2013 as what should have been the perfect team. They had the greatest players at the time in the

---

[168] Roth. 2018.

league and over the course of six years ended up with a mix of players from several teams- most of whom no one had heard of. They had a coach that didn't even drink coffee more than once a day before arriving in Seattle (and later became a coffee shop regular in the city). They didn't win the championship, but they surpassed all predictions of success. The Reign battled hard against North Carolina, prevented Portland from beating them at home games, and never once allowed a game loss to change who they were. The Reign began the league as a mature team and reverse-aged as time went on- and somehow made the best of it.

So if there are any Reign players reading this- or any soccer player in the NWSL or any athlete or non-athlete worried about their future- that is the message I forward to you. Your eventual championship title will never come too late, nor has it come too early. The team can be whatever it decides to be- a team for farming players or a team for achieving victories- and the fans will support it. Athletes can stay or leave the team, and Reign fans will always support them. At the heart of it, Reign fans simply want the best for their athletes- regardless of what teams they end up playing for.

Reign fans still send Carson Pickett suggestions for donut shops in Orlando, and Megan Rapinoe still takes selfies with Merritt Mathias every time she's in North Carolina. Reign fans want to see players find challenge in their careers, play on teams that elevate their athleticism and force them to learn new styles of play, find a team where they can finally feel at home; and- if the athlete finds they don't find any of those- that they have the courage (and the finances) to find a new team and start all over.

Epilogue

"MY POWER" Nija, Beyonce, Busiswa

The 2019 season for the Reign saw a lot of change for both the team and the league. In January 2019, Amanda Duffy became the President of the NWSL- officializing her role as the head executive of the league. Her new role gave her formalized power over executive decisions while maintaining her ability to oversee day-to-day decisions that affect the NWSL.[169] The move paved the way for centralization of power in the league and worked to help level the balance of power between the several teams in the NWSL.

The 2019 FIFA Women's World Cup also helped elevate awareness about the league to generalized audiences who began watching athletes from several women's national teams from around the world play in the US league. The increased awareness of the league also helped attract big-name sponsors including Budweiser who became the official beer sponsor for the NWSL mid-way through the season. The new sponsor even began a campaign for other sponsors to take notice and join the growing league.[170]

While the NWSL lost their television partnership with Lifetime for the 2019 season, they did make a deal with ESPN to televise a thirty games including the post-season- broadening the television audience for the league and increasing the scope of the conversation about women's soccer.[171] The announcement came after the successful viewership for the women's world cup in France during which 1.12 billion viewers watched the several games of the tournament. Roughly one seventh of the entire world's population watched the games.[172]

Not only was there an increase in television viewership, the several teams of the NWSL also received increased in-game attendance. In 2019, the Reign organization announced they would be playing games in Tacoma (roughly an hour's drive south of Seattle) at Cheney Stadium- a minor league baseball team's home

---

[169] **NWSL. 2019.**
[170] **Dosh. 2019.**
[171] **Levine. 2019.**
[172] **FIFA. 2019.**

base (get it?!). The larger stadium and greater awareness paired with higher quality seating and facilities helped grow in-game attendance for the Reign from a season high of roughly 4600 per game in 2016 to roughly 5200 per game in 2019. On a 29 September Cascadia Clash rivalry game, there were roughly 7400 in attendance. The total number of tickets sold for the season numbered at roughly 62,500- surpassing the 2017 record high of 48,500.[173]

"Where Does the Good Go" Tegan and Sara

With a bigger audience, the Reign FC had to maintain their powerful performance into the 2019 season; and they did not disappoint. The team suffered several injuries that forced hastate and rorarii players into leadership roles on the pitch, and those players made themselves into household names among Reign fans. The season's several injuries forced the team and coach Vlatko Andonovski to make mid-season trades and sign free agents to maintain the minimum roster number for the team, but it worked. The Reign made it to the postseason, and played one heck of a game against number one seed North Carolina in the semi-finals before losing in overtime.

Because of the Women's World Cup, several triarii players were out for the majority of the season, and their rorarii replacements played more than usual. Triarii Lydia Williams (Australia) was out for the season due to a combination of the world cup and injury, and principe Michelle Betos was out for nearly the entire season for an injury sustained during the early weeks of the season. Rorarii Casey Murphy quickly rose to hastate status for her unprecedented work as back-up goalkeeper as the Reign team worked hard to find a second athlete to fill the role following rorarii Scout Watson's in-practice injury midway through the season. While the team settled on acquiring Sammy Jo Prudhomme from the Washington Spirit, they maintained Murphy in the goal.

Of the ten defenders on the Reign's 2019 roster, four sustained injuries either before or during the season that forced their withdraw from play- including triarii Steph Catley (Australia), Theresa Nielsen (Denmark), and Celia Jimenez Delgado (Spain); as well as hastati Taylor Smith (acquired from the Washington Spirit).

---

[173] Reign FC. 2019.

The three triarii all returned from injury to play before the end of the season. To fill the gaps, the Reign signed Stephanie Cox as a free agent to return from retirement (from the Reign) to play as a rorarii in the season to replace the injured rorarii Taylor Smith.

Midfielder triarii Rebecca Quinn (Canada), Allie Long (USA), Jess Fishlock (Wales), Rumi Utsugi (Japan), and Rosie White (New Zealand) all had to miss either part or all of the season due to either injury or international play. Morgan Proffitt joined the Reign in 2019 as a rorarii for the team's midfield. Forwards Jaycie Johnson and Jasmyne Spencer both sustained season-ending injuries- forcing rorarii Bethany Balcer and Ifeoma Onumonu to step up and fill the games- and they did not disappoint. Both scored several goals for the team during the season.

Both earned contracts as permanent fixtures in the league with the Reign, and Bethany Balcer earned the Rookie of the Year award from the NWSL. Rorarii Addison Steiner also earned hastati status after appearing in the game in Megan Rapinoe's (USA) absence for both international play and injury and in Jodie Taylor's (England) for international play. New hastati on the team not indoctrinated through rorarii experience included Darian Jenkins (North Carolina Courage), and Shea Groom (Sky Blue FC).

Players that left the team ahead of or during the season were triarii Adriana Leon and Maegan Kelly (Canada), Nahomi Kawasumi (Japan), Elizabeth Addo (Ghana), and Elise Kellond-Knight (Australia). The Reign traded Kawasumi for Groom and Kellond-Knight for Prudhomme; and the team waived Addo. Principe Yael Averbuch was suspended due to ongoing illness, and Kiersten "the Ghost" Dallstream retired. Hastati Alyssa Kleiner retired. The team released their rights to triarii Leon and Kelly; and hastatii Kori Butterfield and Erin Yenney.

In the event that any anthropologist, potential sponsor, badass athlete, or family member who's forgotten my contact information is interested in getting in contact with me; please do! I would love to talk women's sports, feminist anthropology, Wonder Woman comics, favorite flavors of ice cream, etc with all of you! Please send an email to josephwilsonanthro@gmail.com.

Soccer Playlist

"One Touch." Jess Glynne, Jax Jones. *One Touch*. Atlantic Records; 2019.

"Rushing Back" Flume, Vera Blue. *Rushing Back*. Future Classic; 2019.

"Show Me Love." Robin S. *Show Me Love*. Champion Records; 1993.

"That's My Girl." Fifth Harmony. *7/27 (Deluxe)*. Epic Records; 2016.

"On + Off." Maggie Rogers. *Heard It In A Past Life*. Capital Records; 2018.

"Kick It to Me." Sammy Rae. *The Good Life*. Sammy Rae Music; 2018.

"How Much Does Your Love Cost?." Thelma Plum. *Monsters*. Warner Music Australia; 2014.

"The Middle." Zedd, Maren Morris, Grey. *The Middle*. Interscope Records; 2018.

"What About Us." The Saturdays. *What About Us*. Polydor Ltd; 2012.

"Break a Sweat." Becky G. *Break a Sweat*. Kemosabe Record; 2015.

"Star Maps." Aly & AJ. *Sanctuary*. Aly & AJ Music LLC; 2019.

"Summer Girl." HAIM. *Summer Girl*. Columbia Records; 2019.

"Super Critical." The Ting Tings. *Super Critical*. Finca Records; 2014.

"Call Your Girlfriend." Robyn. *Body Talk*. Konichiwa Records; 2010.

"Bad At Love." Halsey. *Hopeless fountain kingdom (Deluxe)*. Astralwerks; 2017.

"October." Alessia Cara. *This Summer*. UMG Recordings, Inc; 2019.

"Home with You." Madison Beer. *As She Pleases*. Access Records; 2018.

"2002." Anne-Marie. *2002*. Warner Music UK; 2018.

"Not Above Love." AlunaGeorge. *I Remember*. Universal Music Operations; 2016.

"Unravel Me." Sabrina Claudio. *About Time*. SC Entertainment, LLC; 2017.

"Beautiful People." Andreya Triana. *Life in Colour*. Hi-Tea Records; 2019.

"MY POWER." Nija, Beyonce, Busiswa. *The Lion King: The Gift.* Columbia Records; 2019.

"Where Does the Good Go." Tegan and Sara. *So Jealous.* Warner Records Inc; 2007.

Works Cited

Aguirre, Michael and McKenna, Kevin. "A brief history of LGBTQ Activism in Seattle." *Civil Rights & Labor History Project*. Center for the Study of the Pacific Northwest; 2016.

Aksamit, Monica. "Who I'm Dating…" *Monica Aksamit*. YouTube; 1 March 2018.

Allen, RJ and Ayala, Erica L. "The NWSL's Sky Blue FC Is Falling Apart, On The Field And Off." *Deadspin*; 8 August 2018.

"Amanda Duffy named President of NWSL." *NWSL*; 15 January 2019.

"Amanda Frisbie." *Sky Blue FC*; 2018.

"Andi Tostanoski- Staff Directory- Hawaii Pacific University." *Hawaii Pacific University*; 2018.

Bakowski, Gregg. "England 1-1 Australia: women's international football friendly- as it happened." *The Guardian*; 9 October 2018.

Balf, Celia. "August Team of the Month." *NWSL*; 31 August 2018.

Balf, Celia. "March Team of the Month." *NWSL*; 6 April 2018.

Balf, Celia. "May Team of the Month." *NWSL*; 6 June 2018.

Balf, Celia. "NWSL community celebrates Pride Month." *NWSL*; 8 June 2018.

Balf, Celia. "NWSL Players participate in Playing for Pride." *NWSL*; 14 June 2018.

Balf, Celia. "Quotes: Amanda Duffy's look at the 2018 NWSL season." *NWSL*; 21 March 2018.

Balf, Celia. "United States, Mexico pick up wins on second day of Group A play." *NWSL*; 7 October 2018.

Bellamy, Aaron. "Boston Breakers dispersal draft results." *Vavel*; 30 January 2018.

Best, Katelyn. "Inside the NWSL Players Association's pragmatic approach to progress, unionization." *The Equalizer*; 24 July 2018.

Bird, Liviu. "Red Stars send Keelin Winters to Reign FC in first NWSL trade." *The Equalizer*; 1 March 2013.

Blue, Kevin and Lauer, Larry. "The 3 C's of Being a Captain." *Michigan State University*. Association for Applied Sports Psychology; 2018.

Borden, Sam. "A U.S. Soccer Star's Declaration of Independence." *The New York Times*; 10 April 2013.

Brodeur, Nicole. "Bill Predmore: 'My goal is to build the best women's club in the world'." *Seattle Times*; 3 February 2013.
Camber, Amy. "Reign FC Comics: Barnes." *Seattle Reign FC*; 11 July 2018.
Camber, Amy. "Reign FC Comics: Yanez." *Seattle Reign FC*; 5 June 2018.
"Celebrating 10 Years." *Westfield W-League*; 2018.
"Changing The Definition Of Femininity." *Elle*; 16 November 2016.
Conheeney, Kelly. "Over and Over again." Soccer Girl Probs; 30 July 2018.
Cristobal, Jacob. "Reign FC Original: Christine Nairn." *Sounder At Heart*. SB Nation; 3 May 2017.
Cristobal, Jacob. "Reign FC Original: Jess Fishlock." *Sounder At Heart*. SB Nation; 8 May 2017.
Cristobal, Jacob. "Reign FC Original: Lauren Barnes." *Sounder At Heart*. SB Nation; 20 April 2017.
Cristobal, Jacob. "Reign FC owner responds to report of 'unsustainable losses'." *Sounder At Heart*. SB Nation; 22 September 2017.
Cristobal, Jacob. "Seattle Reign FC will remain at Memorial Stadium for 2019 NWSL season." *Sounder At Heart*. SB Nation; 16 August 2018.
Cristobal, Jacob. "The curious case of Seattle Reign FC's attendance." *Sounder At Heart*. SB Nation; 7 August 2017.
Dosh, Kristi. "Budweiser Launches Campaign To Find New NWSL Spnsors." *Forbes*; 24 October 2019.
"Do you follow major league baseball or not?" *Statista*; 2014.
Eckford, Ryan. "The rise of Olympic footballer Emily van Egmond." *ABC Newcastle*. ABC News; 15 July 2016.
"Emily Zurrer." *Canada Soccer*; 2018.
"England Defeats France 4-1 to Open 2018 SheBelieves Cup." *US Soccer*; 1 March 2018.
"English Civil Wars." *History.com*. A&E Television Networks; 2018.
Erdkamp, Paul. "A Companion to the Roman Army." *John Wiley & Sons*; 31 March 2011.
Farley, Richard. "NWSL: Other general managers should probably stop taking Laura Harvey's calls." *NBC Sports*. NBC; 21 November 2013.

Farley, Richard. "Pregnant Amy Rodriguez to miss NWSL season." *NBC Sports*. NBC; 30 January 2013.

Farley, Richard. "Rules and restrictions define NWSL 'Free Agency'." *NBC Sports*. NBC; 26 January 2013.

FIFA Women's World Cup 2019 watched by more that 1 billion." *FIFA*; 18 October 2019.

Flowe, Charlie. "From the Treadmill to the Pitch: Jenny Ruiz, Seattle Reign FC." *World Sports Show*; 30 April 2013.

"Former Alabama Soccer Player Victoria Frederick Earns Spot with Seattle Reign." *University of Alabama*; 22 April 2013.

"Fortune Favors the Bold." *Reign Academy*. Seattle Reign FC; 2018.

Foxhoven, Danielle. "Pro Skills Soccer." *Danielle Foxhoven: The Official Website of Danielle Foxhoven*; 2018.

Gabriel, Cassidy. "July Team of the Month." *NWSL*; 3 August 2018.

"Get Statistics." *NSVRC*; 2018.

Goldberg, Jamie. "Portland Thorns coach Mark Parsons has suspension overturned, will coach in home opener." *The Oregonian*; 6 April 2018.

Goldberg, Jamie. "Portland Thorns defender Meghan Klingenberg suspended for kicking Seattle's Allie Long." *The Oregonian*; 5 July 2018.

"Haley Kopmeyer." *MGOBlue*. University of Michigan; 2018.

Halloran, John D. "Amanda Duffy Addresses NWSL Present and Future." *American Soccer Now*; 8 May 2017.

Harris, Ashlyn. "Today is World Suicide Prevention Day." *Ashlyn Harris*. Instagram; 10 September 2018.

"Havana Solaun." *Washington Spirit*; 2018.

Hawbaker, KT and Johnson, Christen A. "#MeToo: A timeline of events." *Chicago Tribune*; 20 August 2018.

"Big Game Days in College Football Linked With Sexual Assault." *Heavy*; 20 September 2018.

"Japan: The Tokugawa (1600-1868)." *Asia for Educators*. Columbia University; 2009.

Jarrett, Natalee. "Aussies on the Rise: The Growth of Women in Sports in Australia." The She Network. Women's Sports Foundation; 4 December 2017.

"Hope Solo Biography." *Biography.com*. A&E Entertainment; 2 April 2014.

"Houston Dash Re-Sign Defender Amber Brooks." *Houston Dash*; 25 January 2018.

Kassouf, Jeff. "PRO assured accountability, NWSL coaches have reached breaking point over referees." *The Equilizer*; 25 July 2018.

"Keelin Winters on Her Post-Soccer Career as a Firefighter." *Seattle Reign FC*. The Bold 18 May 2018.

Kenner, Ali. "Necessary Evils." *Cultural Anthropology*; 28 April 2017.

"Kiersten Dallstream Profile The Washington State University Official Athletic Site." *Washington State University*; 18 April 2013.

King, Rachel C. "2014 NWSL Expansion Draft Results." *NWSL*. Pitchside Report; 2013.

Klein, Robby. "USWNT's Christen Press signs with club in Sweden after NWSL holdout." *ESPNW*. ESPN; 26 March 2018.

"K. Larsen." *SoccerWay*; 2018.

Kyle, Kaylyn. "Who I Am." *KaylynKyleSoccer.com*; 2015.

Lauletta, Dan. "FOX Sports to air six NWSL matches on FS1." *The Equalizer*; 14 April 2016.

Lauletta, Dan. "Reign make two trades, land Cuellar for Noyola." *The Equalizer*; 1 July 2013.

Lee, Maddie. "Utah Royals acquire U.S. forward Christen Press in team trade." *The Salt Lake Tribune*; 18 June 2018.

Levine, Matthew. "ESPN signs exclusive multimedia agreement for worldwide rights to the National Women's Soccer League regular season matches." *NWSL*; 16 August 2019.

Linehan, Meg. "Liz Bogus tapped as assistant coach for Utah women's soccer." *Excelle Sports*; 31 January 2017.

"Lyndsey Patterson Joins Seattle Reign FC." *Sounder At Heart*. SB Nation; 28 February 2013.

Mandell, Nina. "WPS, second attempt at a professional women's soccer league in the U.S., officially folds after three seasons." *Daily News*. New York Daily News; 18 May 2012.

"Marist's First Female Professional Soccer Player-Kristen Meier." *Marist School*; 8 April 2013.

Marsh, Sarah. "The pressure of perfection: five women tell their stories." *The Guardian*; 14 October 2016.

Mayers, Joshua. "Reign FC announces roster for 2013 season." *Sounders FC Blog*. The Seattle Times; 27 April 2017.

McCann, Allison. "Low Pay Limits Player Experience in National Women's Soccer League." *Five Thirty Eight*; 24 March 2014.

McCausland, Phil and Silva, Daniella. "Serena Williams' U.S. Open penalties spark debate over sexism in sports." *NBC News*. NBC; 9 September 2018.

McIntyre, Doug. "Red, White and Green: Duel Citizens Suit Up For Mexico's National Team." *ESPNW*. ESPN; 6 June 2015.

"Meet Soccer Superstar: Lauren Barnes." *Nuzest*; 2018.

"Michelle Betos Drafted By Seattle Reign." *University of Georgia Athletics. University of Georgia*; 7 February 2013.

Miller, Gretchen; Scheyer, Jonathan; and Sherrard, Emily. "Women's United Soccer League." *Duke University*; 2018.

Moscato, Carmelina. "Carmelina Moscato." *Western Sydney Wanderers FC*; 13 October 2015.

Neighmond, Patti. "Benefits Of Sports To A Child's Mind And Heart All Part Of The Game." *Shots: Health News from NPR*. NPR; 1 July 2015.

"NWSL Announces Supplemental Draft and Discovery Player Process." *Boston Breakers*. Boston Women's Soccer; 2013.

"NWSL Statement on Discriminatory Legislation." *LGBT Soccer*; 14 March 2017.

"NWSL Supplemental Draft Results." *Pitchside Report*; 2013.

Oshan, Jeremiah. "Reign Swap Draft Pick For Winters in 1st Ever NWSL Trade." *Sounder At Heart*. SB Nation; 1 March 2013.

Oshan, Jeremiah. "Seattle Reign sign four free agents: Kate Deines, Jess Fishlock, Tiffany Cameron, Lindsay Taylor." *Sounder At Heart*. SB Nation; 4 February 2013.

Oxenham, Gwendolyn. "Under the Lights and Into the Dark." Print. *Icon*. Clays Ltd; 2017.

"Partnerships." *ReignFC.com*. Seattle Reign FC; 2018.

"Party Whips." *United States Senate*; 2018.

Perez, AJ. "American gymnasts detail sexual abuse to legislators on Capitol Hill." *USA Today*; 1 March 2018.

"Player Spotlight: Carson Pickett (Orlando Pride)." *Lifetime*. YouTube 7 July 2018.

"Player Spotlight: Jessica Fishlock (Seattle Reign)." *Lifetime*. YouTube; 31 July 2018.

"Player Spotlight: Lydia Williams (Seattle Reign)." *Lifetime*. YouTube 17 September 2018.

"Players." *Stats*. NWSL; 2018.

"Pride Games To Support Include Storm, Reign and Mariners." *Seattle Gay Scene*; 15 June 2018.

Purdy, Jacqueline. "April Team of the Month." *NWSL*; 3 May 2018.

Purdy, Jacqueline. "Arin Gilliland injury update." *NWSL*; 15 July 2018.

Purdy, Jacqueline. "Canada roster set for Concacaf Women's Championship." *NWSL*; 26 September 2018.

Purdy, Jacqueline. "Henninger, Johnson, Murillo named to Mexico roster for Concacaf Women's Championship." *NWSL*; 26 September 2018.

Purdy, Jacqueline. "Japan, Australia name rosters for 2018 Tournament of Nations." *NWSL*; 17 July 2018.

Purdy, Jacqueline. "Johnson, Henninger and Mexico win 2018 Central American and Caribbean Games." *NWSL*; 31 July 2018.

Purdy, Jacqueline. "June Team of the Month." *NWSL*; 6 June 2018.

Purdy, Jacqueline. "Kerr scores again in Australia's wild win over Norway; Full Algarve Cup and Cyprus Cup results." *NWSL*; 28 February 2018.

Purdy, Jacqueline. "Leon scores four as Canada picks up 12-0 win over Cuba; Jamaica beats Costa Rica 1-0." *NWSL*; 8 October 2018.

Purdy, Jacqueline. "Preview: Seattle Reign FC." *NWSL*; 19 March 2018.

Purdy, Jacqueline. "Prince scores twice as Canada opens up World Cup qualifying with 2-0 win over Jamaica." *NWSL;* 5 October 2018.

Purdy, Jacqueline. "Schedule & Results: NWSL on international duty." *NWSL*; 11 April 2018.

Purdy, Jacqueline. "Schedule & Results: NWSL on international duty in June." *NWSL*; 11 June 2018.

Purdy, Jacqueline. "Seven NWSL players on Brazil's Tournament of Nations roster." *NWSL*; 23 July 2018.

Purdy, Jacqueline. "SheBelieves Cup: United States, England win on Day 1." *NWSL*; 1 March 2018.

Purdy, Jacqueline. "SheBelieves Cup: United States, France tie 1-1; Germany, England also tie." *NWSL*; 4 March 2018.

Purdy, Jacqueline. "Sinclair scores No 170; Algarve, Cyprus Cup results." *NWSL*; 2 March 2018.

Purdy, Jacqueline. "Sinclair scores twice in Canada's win at the Algarve Cup; More international results." *NWSL*; 6 March 2018.

Purdy, Jacqueline. "Switzerland and the Netherlands advance to final play-off for UEFA's final World Cup berth." *NWSL*; 9 October 2018.

Purdy, Jacqueline. "Twenty-four NWSL players on UWSNT training camp roster ahead of Tournament of Nations." *NWSL*; 18 July 2018.

Purdy, Jacqueline. "UEFA play-offs schedule & results; Schedule of NWSL players on international duty." *NWSL*; 5 October 2018.

Purdy, Jacqueline. "US Names 20-woman roster for Concacaf Women's Championship." *NWSL*; 19 September 2018.

Purdy, Jacqueline. "Week 1 Rewind: We're back!" *NWSL*; 26 March 2018.

Purdy, Jacqueline. "Week 19 Power Standings: Courage Still No. 1, every other team changes spots." *NWSL*; 6 August 2018.

Purdy, Jacqueline. "2018 NWSL GM Survey." *NWSL*; 12 March 2018.

Purdy, Jacqueline. "2018 NWSL Media Survey." *NWSL*; 13 March 2018.

Rantz, Susie. "Power Ranking: NWSL Team Jerseys." *Seattle Reign FC*. The Bold; 9 April 2015.

"Reign FC Break Club Attendance Records in 2019." *Reign FC*; 3 October 2019.

"Reign FC Legend: Leigh Morgan." *Seattle Reign FC*. The Bold; 14 June 2017.

Roberson, Matthew. "Seattle's Season Comes to an End with First-Round Loss at Phoenix." *Seattle Storm*. WNBA; 7 September 2017.

"Roster Rules." *NWSL*; 2018.

Roth, Eric. "The Curious Case of Benjamin Button." Film. *The Kennedy/Marshall Company*. Paramount Pictures; 2008.

Rothenberg, Ben. "Tennis Star Petra Kvitova Badly Injured in Home Invasion." *The New York Times*; 20 December 2016.

"Seattle Reign FC Acquire Steph Catley and Jasmyne Spencer from Orlando Pride." *Seattle Reign FC*; 29 January 2018.

"Seattle Reign FC Sign Forward Jaycie Johnson as National Team Replacement Player." *Seattle Reign FC*. The Bold; 30 March 2018.

Sheinin, Dave. "London swimming star Missy Franklin in danger of not making Rio team." *The Washington Post*; 29 June 2016.

Sibor, Doug. "The 25 Strangest Trades in Sports History." *Complex Media*; 10 March 2014.

Soper, Taylor. "Microsoft inks deal with Seattle Reign soccer team for jersey sponsorship." *Geek Wire*; 7 April 2016.

"Spirit acquire forward Lindsay Taylor from Seattle." *Washington Spirit*; 1 July 2013.

Steinbach, Paul. "Spectator Venues Are Realizing the Benefits of Downsizing Seating Capacity." *Athletic Business*; June 2015.

Tannenwald, Jonathan. "Jessica McDonald nearly quit soccer, now she's NWSL champion, MVP." *Pro Soccer USA*; 24 September 2018.

"The World of the Ancient Romans- Warfare." *The Ancient World*; 2018.

Torres, Aaron. "Portland Thorns fan support is unlike anything else in women's soccer." *The Washington Post*; 24 June 2017.

"USA Head Coach Jill Ellis Names 2016 U.S. Olympic Women's Soccer Team." *US Soccer*; 12 July 2016.

"U.S. Soccer Bio-Banding Initiative." *U.S. Soccer*. YouTube; 20 April 2018.

"USWNT celebrates life of Alyssa Alhadeff with her family and friends." *ESPNW*. ESPN; 2018.

"Utah Royals FC add Scotland Captain DF Rachel Corsie to Inaugural Season Roster." *Utah Royals FC*; 19 March 2018.

Vagianos, Alanna. "ESPN's Body Issue Features An Openly Gay Couple For The First Time." *Huffington Post*; 26 June 2018.

Valentine, Julia. "Seattle Reign defender Elli Reed is living (and sharing) the dream." *SocCity*; 19 September 2017.

"Vlatko Andonovski on His Journey to 50 NWSL Wins." *Seattle Reign FC*. The Bold; 12 May 2018.

Wamsley, Laurel. "Equal Pay for Equal Shreds: World Surf League Will Award Same Prizes To Men And Women." *NPR Sports*. NPR; 7 September 2018.

"Water1st International & Seattle Reign FC Form Partnership to Reduce Water Access Challenges for World's Poorest." *Water1st International*; 3 February 2016.

"Week 7 Power Rankings: Big wins for Courage, Reign and Pride earn this week's top spots." *NWSL*; 14 May 2018.

"Week 13 Power Rankings: Courage back to winnings, Pride move up to No. 2." *NWSL*; 25 June 2018.

"Week 14 Power Rankings: No budge at the top as the Courage hold on; Reign FC move to No. 2." *NWSL*; 2 July 2018.

"Western Sydney Wanderers preview." *Western Sydney Wanderers*; 26 October 2016.

"Will Lemoore Open Another Door for Women?" *World Surf League*; 22 September 2017.

"Women's Soccer Staff Adds Alum Elli Reed as Director of Operations." *University of Portland*; 1 February 2018.

Wulff, Alexia. "How Portland Became America's Capital of 'Weird' and Embrace It." *Culture Trip*; 29 January 2017.

Yuval-Davis, Nira. "Belonging and the politics of belonging." *Patterns of Prejudice*; Volume 40 Issue 3. Taylor & Francis Online; 5 August 2006.

Zemler, Emily. "12 Times Women Competed Against Men- And Won." *Elle*; 14 August 2017.

Zuniga, Alejandro. "After preseason, Reign already used to road trips." *The Equalizer*; 17 April 2013.

"2013 NWSL Draft Results." *ESNN*. Top Drawer Soccer; 18 January 2013.

"2017 NWSL Attendance." *Soccer Stadium Digest*; 2017.

"2018 Best XI and Second XI announced." *NWSL*; 20 September 2018.

"2018 NWSL College Draft: Full Broadcast." *NWSL*. YouTube; 19 Jan 2018.

"2018 Reign FC Season Ticket Holder Kickoff Event- Interview: Bev Yanez & Lauren Barnes." *Seattle Reign FC*. YouTube; 22 March 2018.

"2018 Reign FC Season Ticket Holder Kickoff Event- Interview: Vlatko Andonovski." *Seattle Reign FC*. YouTube; 22 March 2018.

"#MakeWavesMoveMountains." *Roxy Pro*; 14 March 2018.

Made in the USA
Las Vegas, NV
09 May 2024